BLAISDELL '51

THE *REAL BOOK* ABOUT
GEORGE
WASHINGTON

THE *REAL BOOK* ABOUT

GEORGE
WASHINGTON

BY

HAROLD COY

Illustrated by

ELINORE BLAISDELL

EDITED BY HELEN HOKE

Garden City Books

GARDEN CITY, NEW YORK

BY ARRANGEMENT WITH FRANKLIN WATTS, INC.

1952

GARDEN CITY BOOKS

PRINTED IN THE UNITED STATES

Contents

Chapter 1	A WORLD TO SEE	9
Chapter 2	A WORLD TO WIN	17
Chapter 3	A WILDERNESS TO CHART	25
Chapter 4	HEIR OF LAWRENCE	32
Chapter 5	MESSENGER TO THE FRENCH	40
Chapter 6	TOO LITTLE, TOO LATE	49
Chapter 7	REDCOATS AND BUCKSKINS	59
Chapter 8	PATIENCE AND REWARD	68
Chapter 9	MOUNT VERNON'S NO. 1 FARMER	77
Chapter 10	A TIME FOR SPEECHES	85
Chapter 11	A TIME FOR ACTION	95
Chapter 12	A VIRGINIAN AMONG THE YANKEES	105
Chapter 13	FREE AND INDEPENDENT STATES	114
Chapter 14	FOOTPRINTS IN THE SNOW	123

Chapter 15 CAN SPRING BE FAR BEHIND? 131

Chapter 16 THE WORLD TURNED UPSIDE
          DOWN   140

Chapter 17 BACK TO THE FARM   151

Chapter 18 THE NEW ROOF   159

Chapter 19 TWO PARTIES   168

Chapter 20 FAREWELL AT LAST   177

          REAL DATES IN THE LIFE OF
          GEORGE WASHINGTON   185

          INDEX   189

THE *REAL BOOK* ABOUT
GEORGE
WASHINGTON

Chapter 1: A WORLD TO SEE

"STAND BACK! Your mother would never forgive me if harm came to her first-born."

At his father's command, the boy stepped back from the furnace door, shielding his eyes from the ball of glowing metal. George had never seen anything so dazzling in his five and a half years of life.

He had watched the workmen, under his father's orders, shoveling in the layers of charcoal and clay until the tall furnace was full. At first it made a feeble blaze. Then mighty blasts of air from the bellows fed the flames. Now there was only a molten mass.

So this was how iron was made!

In the fiery glow George's chestnut hair, tapering into a pigtail, appeared redder than it really was. The workmen saw that the ironmaster's son was large for his age.

"He will be a tall man like his father," remarked one of them.

"Yes, and strong," said his companion.

George wiped his fair cheeks. Sweat dripped on his Indian hunting shirt, but the keen gray-blue eyes were not missing a thing. Now his father was tapping the furnace. The hissing metal rushed out in a liquid stream. George watched him guide it into molds to cool.

Life had been full of excitement since his father's return from England. There were many gifts, among them a tea cart for his mother, a tool chest for him and toy birds for his little sister and baby brothers. There were greetings from his half brothers Lawrence and Austin, who would be coming home from school in England.

In his father's long absence George had grown fast. Now he was big enough to visit the furnace. They had started early, for the road was long. The wagon bumped through the woods. It bogged down in creeks and marshes until Augustine Washington declared he would seek a new home for his family, handier to the ironworks.

Finally, late in the day, they loaded the wagon.

George was proud to see how easily his father lifted a mass of iron that two other men had to struggle to get off the floor.

The final adventure of this happy summer day was the trip to the river landing. Then they would put up for the night with friends. In friendly Virginia they were sure of a welcome wherever they stopped.

"Father, what will happen to this iron?" asked George.

"It will be shipped to England. Each ton I lay down at the wharf will bring me twenty shillings. With tobacco fetching a wretched price, and English goods so dear, I can make use of the money."

Father and son rode on in silence. The shadows gathered. Finally Mr. Washington spoke.

"If all goes well, you will see England one day, too. There you will receive a gentleman's education, like Lawrence and Austin. Meanwhile, we must find a school in Virginia where at least you can learn to cipher and write a fair hand. Another reason for us to move!"

As George moved closer to the tall figure beside him in the darkness, he tried to imagine what these new adventures would be like.

"In February," he reminded himself, "I shall be six years old."

Why, now that George Washington was growing up—anything could happen!

Before George's seventh birthday the Washington family did move. It was the boy's third home. He had little memory of his birthplace on Bridges Creek, far down the Potomac River. It was near the farm where his great-grandfather settled upon moving from England long ago.

George's second home was a hundred miles up the Potomac. Even here, the river was like an arm of the sea. English ships could anchor right in front of the Washington plantation.

Now the Washingtons were to live beside another river, the Rappahannock. The part of Virginia between these two rivers was called the Northern Neck. George had wondered whether the new river would be like the Potomac. He was disappointed at first to see how narrow it was.

"I bet I can throw a stone across that old river when I am as old as Lawrence!" he exclaimed.

However, the new place was near the ironworks. There was more room for the growing Washington family. Lawrence was back from England now, a young man of spirit and fine manners. In the younger set, besides George, there were Betty, Sam, Jack and baby Charlie. The red frame house, two stories high, had brick chimneys at either end to draw off the smoke from the huge fireplaces inside. Small buildings clustered about the big house. These included the sheds, barns, stables, and tobacco houses. The kitchen and washhouse were set apart where they would not heat up the living quarters. Then there were the cabins of the Negro slaves who worked in the fields.

It looked like a little village, but it was really a family establishment like many others of the time. The Washingtons called it Ferry Farm. That was because of the ferry crossing at the foot of the hill.

George loved to cross the river on the little boat. He saw horses and riders bound for distant places. Just to stop on the opposite shore was exciting, for here was Fredericksburg. It was a real town—the first George had ever seen. Many houses stood on a hill, while below there were a courthouse, a church, a stone prison and all the shops. George's favorite was the apothecary's shop. Here, for a halfpenny, he could buy a piece of brown-sugar candy.

Best of all, he liked the tobacco warehouses and the wharf. Planters from the back country rolled their tobacco down to the little port in hogsheads.

Everyone complained about the low prices the London merchants paid for tobacco. Their hopes of making money lay elsewhere. They were hunting for bargains in the unsettled lands beyond the Blue Ridge Mountains, where the Indian warpaths lay. With new settlers arriving, this was going to be a big country someday. A man smart enough to mark out a few thousand acres for himself in the right spot would live to be rich. George listened closely. He heard the same kind of talk from his father, so it must be true. Maybe he was wrong to squander his pennies on brown-sugar candy. By saving them he could buy land.

The Fredericksburg wharf was a meeting place. Weather-beaten sailors from three-masted English ships boasted of battling fierce pirates on the high seas. Bearded trappers in coonskin caps led their pack horses there—loaded with furs from the Indian country.

A rough-spoken man was shipping a bundle of beaver skins to London. He complained that, though he was poorly paid, the fur would come back as expensive beaver hats for Virginia gentlemen. The skins, he said, could just as well be turned into hats right here in Virginia if it weren't for that crazy law. He meant the one that said His Majesty's subjects in the American colonies couldn't make anything that hurt the trade of the mother country.

Someone protested. "The King's soldiers protect us from the Indians, and the English trade pays the cost."

"Faugh! Where I came from, a man protects himself." The trapper patted the rifle at his side.

To all this the growing boy listened. He seldom said a word. But he never missed a word.

George made another discovery on the banks of the Rappahannock. He came to know his growing strength and skill. He was a good swimmer. In pitching horseshoes his aim was sure. He could hurl an iron bar farther than any boy his age. Best of all, George, at eight, was a fine "rassler." He could down the best of them if he were anywhere near their size.

Families were large in those days, so every child had plenty of aunts and uncles. From his Uncle Ben, George received a dapple-gray pony named Hero.

"Now I can get together with the other boys who have ponies. We'll have a horse race!" he cried.

"Indeed you won't, young man!" His mother's voice was stern. "You will ride your pony only when a grownup goes along and leads him by the bridle."

"But Hero is a gentle pony, Mother."

"No mind, I won't have you getting hurt."

This slow pace annoyed George, for he liked to have his way. Nevertheless, the strict Mary Washington had taught her son obedience. So he swallowed his disappointment, dreaming of the day when he would be old enough to break the wildest horses.

George loved to go with his father on fishing and hunting trips. They would come back loaded with shad or wild turkeys. In the woods he took his turn with the ax, cutting away girdles of bark so the forest trees would die and make room for new tobacco plantings.

George got plenty of exercise this way. So he wasn't tempted to cut down his father's cherry tree, despite the story that later got around. Of course,

Augustine Washington did have a fine orchard. Besides cherries, it bore apples—and so many peaches that he fed them to the hogs.

By the time George was nine years old all he could think about was a soldier's life. His brother Lawrence, a captain, had sailed off to fight the King's enemies on the Spanish Main. No wonder George's blood tingled as letters came from Lawrence. No wonder he had his schoolmates marching to the drumbeat of a gourd and carrying cornstalks for muskets.

The school George went to was conducted by the Anglican minister in Fredericksburg. Every now and then his father paid a hundred pounds of tobacco for the lessons. There was little money in Virginia. People earned tobacco for their work. They didn't have to smoke their wages, though. They got a piece of paper saying their tobacco was in a warehouse. This they could sell or use for money.

The dancing master was paid in tobacco, too. He went from plantation to plantation, teaching the children country dances and the minuet. With George's heart now set on being a soldier, however, he had little taste for putting on a velvet coat and shoes with silver buckles and stepping and bowing to a fiddler's tune.

He had to, though. His mother declared, "No son of mine is going to grow up to be a blunderbuss in a drawing room."

Chapter 2: A WORLD TO WIN

IN 1742 GEORGE was ten years old. It was a big year.
His brothers were older and more fun to play with.
Betty was a big girl and looked enough like George to
be his twin. Austin came home from Appleby School
in England. George could hardly wait to go there,
too. He hoped an English education would make him
a man of the world like the gracious Austin and, most
of all, a fearless soldier like Lawrence.

It was Lawrence's return from war with Spain on
the treasure coast of South America that made this
a year never to be forgotten. George saw it as the
homecoming of a conquering hero. Augustine Wash-

ington had a father's pride, but he knew all too well that his son's hollow eyes had looked upon suffering and defeat.

Indeed, more than half of Lawrence's comrades-in-arms had perished—some from enemy cannonading, more from disease. After battering to Cartagena's inner harbor the expedition had failed. The survivors had to turn back.

"If the advice of our gallant Admiral Vernon had been followed, the gold of Cartagena would be ours." Sadly Lawrence shook his head. "But the commander of the land forces General Wentworth moved all too slowly. The ships tore holes in the walls, but he found a hundred excuses to delay. When finally he tried to push through, the foe was well prepared. To make matters worse, the rainy season came. Then fever did the rest."

Lawrence's sunken cheeks flushed. "Wentworth has only scorn for us colonials. It was Vernon's plea that the castle be quickly stormed. But the general looked upon us as cowards without discipline. He thinks only his precious red-coated soldiers trained in Britain can face fire with courage."

Lawrence Washington's eyes flashed. "I believe a Virginian to be as capable of serving his King with honor as any redcoat. Yet we remained cooped up aboard ship. We were short of food and water. All we could do was watch our companions die like flies."

George was indignant that his brave half brother should be so ill treated. He felt better when Lawrence became a major of Virginia's militia and was drilling the men for the colony's defense.

Washington was becoming a respected family name in Virginia. Augustine kept shipping more iron and tobacco to England. As often as he could he bought more land, hoping to make all his sons well off. George was taught how to draw a bill of sale and a promissory note, how to measure land, how to compute compound interest. He was good at figures.

During the Easter season of 1743 George was allowed a holiday to visit his Washington cousins on the Chotank shore of the Potomac. The world looked bright. The trees were in leaf. There would be horse racing before his return.

The pleasant vacation was interrupted by a messenger from Ferry Farm. George must return at once. His father was very ill. When George reached home the tall frame of Augustine Washington lay helpless on a feather bed. He was breathing his last. The end came soon.

Mr. Washington was only forty-nine. He had not lived long enough to make all his dreams come true. His grieving widow collected her brood of five, from eleven-year-old George to Charlie, not quite five.

"We are poor now," said Mary Washington, "and you must not expect things you might have looked for had your father lived." She turned to George. "You are my eldest. You are the man of the family."

By the custom of the time, most of what Augustine Washington had went to his eldest son Lawrence. It was for him to keep bright the luster of the family name. To Austin went the down-river plantation that was George's birthplace. Smaller farms were to belong to the other children when they grew up.

George, as the oldest of his father's "second family," was to have Ferry Farm when he came of age—together with ten slaves. Meanwhile, his mother would have the use of her children's property along with her own. It was not a rich legacy. But it was something. What George could make of it was up to him. As it turned out, George's best legacy was something not mentioned in the will at all. Rummaging in a dark closet among his father's things one day, he came upon a set of surveyor's instruments. Here was a compass, a tripod—and also the poles and chains used in marking off land. Such equipment was useful indeed in this new country.

"I will learn how to survey land," George promised himself. He set himself to arithmetic with new determination.

Lawrence admired the manly spirit and ambition he saw in his younger brother. He did all he could to take a father's place.

Lawrence was now building a fine home on the Potomac estate, where the family had lived before moving to the Rappahannock. The name he chose for it honored the great admiral on whose flagship he had served. It was called Mount Vernon.

All doors were open to a handsome soldier like Lawrence—even those of Belvoir, where the Fairfaxes lived. Colonel Fairfax managed the Virginia property of his cousin Lord Fairfax. It was said that this powerful English lord owned not less than five million acres in Virginia. Colonel Fairfax had a gracious and beautiful daughter named Anne. In the summer of 1743 she became Lawrence's bride.

George was welcome at Mount Vernon whenever his mother would let him go. The same welcome awaited him at the place down the Potomac, where Austin settled and married. George's cousins were glad to see him, too. So the lad entered his teens with four places he could call his home.

After his thirteenth birthday, George began shooting up to a man's height. Lawrence thought of the splendid Admiral Vernon. Why wouldn't the sea be just the place for a youth of George's mettle to make a name for himself? It did not take long for George's imagination to be fired, too. He dreamed of sailing before the mast and rising in the King's navy.

George's mother thought otherwise. She didn't want her son sailing off into the unknown dangers of the sea. Lawrence reasoned with his stepmother. So did other people. Finally Mary Washington was almost convinced. George packed a sea bag, eager to be a sailor. At the last minute a letter came from George's uncle in London—his mother's brother.

"Don't let George go to sea," it said. "They will treat him like a dog. He will have little chance to become an officer. As a colonial he is without influence. Even as a humble farmer he will be better off."

Mary Washington told her son to unpack.

George's career at sea ended before it began.

The ship sailed off without George. But he thought of his father's surveying instruments and was consoled. Whenever he met a surveyor he pestered him with questions. He gladly carried the man's poles and chains—just for a chance to go along.

George neatly copied whatever he learned into his exercise book. It was not easy to be a good surveyor, however. Among the problems were "how to measure a piece of ground be it ever so irregular."

When George visited Mount Vernon just after his sixteenth birthday, he set up his instruments in a turnip patch and made careful notes. From these he prepared a chart, true to scale. Below he wrote in a clear hand, "A Plan of Major Lawrence Washington's Turnip Field as Surveyed by Me"—and signed himself "G.W." in bold initials.

Bursting with pride, George ran up to his brother's fashionable friends at their afternoon card playing to show his work. The guests were surprised to see how neat, accurate and thorough it was.

About this time George earned his first money, two pounds and three shillings, for helping a Fredericksburg surveyor. He knew what he was going to do with that money. He put it aside. He had spotted some fine pieces of land on his trips.

So George was making progress. Yet on measuring himself against the dark and slender Lawrence, with his gift for always saying the right thing, the raw-boned youth felt ill at ease. When he asked a young lady for a dance, his big feet seemed to trip him up. Behind their fans, he suspected, the girls were tittering at his awkwardness.

The one thing he could do well in this polite society was ride to hounds. When the horns sounded at break of day, the daring George was off at breakneck speed across the fields with the best of them.

Knowing he would have to be self-taught from now on, he searched the library at Mount Vernon for books to learn from. One, a volume Lawrence had used at school, contained one hundred and ten "Rules of Civility and Decent Behavior in Company and Conversation."

Here, thought George, is just what I have been looking for. Maybe he couldn't ever attend an English school. But he would do his best to become a gentleman anyway.

Seizing a quill he sat down to copy the rules into his exercise book—good rules, teaching that consideration for others underlies all polite manners.

Some were aimed at the cruder customs of the day. George learned that he shouldn't spit into the fire, or speak with meat in his mouth or clean his teeth with the tablecloth.

"Be no flatterer," read another rule. Well, he guessed it wasn't his nature to say things he didn't mean. Thoughtfully the boy continued writing:

"Let your countenance be pleasant but in serious matters somewhat grave.

"Show not yourself glad at the misfortune of another, though he may be your enemy.

"When a man does all he can, though it succeed not well, blame not him that did it."

At this George reminded himself, "That's right, all I can do is my best. These are surely fine rules for a gentleman to live by always."

His arm grew weary, but he kept on until he had copied the very last rule of all:

"Labor to keep alive in your breast that little spark of celestial fire called Conscience."

Chapter 3: A WILDERNESS TO CHART

GEORGE couldn't have been more excited if he were about to visit the King. Lord Fairfax had arrived at Belvoir to take a look at his vast New World domain. He *was* a king—in America, at least. Just the fine clothes he had with him, when the ship dropped anchor in the Potomac, were said to fill a score of chests. His appearance would surely put to shame these colonial planters.

George was to be at the reception for Lord Fairfax. He knew he would cut a poor figure before such elegance. The best thing for him was to let his elders talk and, if spoken to, give a straightforward answer.

Society of the Northern Neck—for counties around—was at the Fairfax mansion. All were straining for their first view of the great nobleman—the ladies in sweeping silken gowns, the gentlemen in powdered wigs, knee breeches and coats with flowing tails. George kept in the background.

But who was the unkempt figure who now appeared amid this splendor? The stranger had a ragged beard. There was not even a ruffle at his collar—and he wore coarse linen breeches and a threadbare coat.

A sensation ran through the drawing room when it was learned that this was none other than the great Lord Fairfax himself! What in the world had happened to all those fine clothes of his?

Fairfax, a large, swarthy man past fifty, was indifferent to the excitement he was causing. Avoiding the company of the ladies, he retired to a back room. There he was drawn into a game of dominoes. Before long he yawned, moved over to an easy chair and buried himself in a book.

George was astonished. Lawrence, passing by, whispered, "Don't be surprised. He's an odd character—but the soul of generosity to those he likes."

At fox hunting next morning His Lordship showed his first enthusiasm. Here was something he could put his heart into! He was given the best mount and was a splendid horseman besides. With the dogs in full cry he quickly led the pursuit. George was not far behind. He was at Lord Fairfax's side as the frightened fox was treed.

Apart from the others, the pair rode back from the kill. Fairfax looked at George and spoke.

"You are a true huntsman, my boy. You ride superbly."

George stammered out thanks. His Lordship continued. "You must be nearly twenty. I suppose you are thinking of settling down and marrying."

"I am only sixteen, sir. And I fear I am far from popular with the ladies."

"Pshaw! There's no accounting for a woman's taste. A fair lady in London jilted me to marry a duke. Don't give the ladies a second thought, son."

And Fairfax turned his gaze to the western horizon as if the rolling acres belonged to him—as in fact they mostly did.

"It is time my lands were bounded and my claims made secure," he said. "Besides, I am going to build myself a home out there—out in the forest, away from London with its fickle women and false values."

The great landowner didn't say much else on the ride back to Belvoir. Only this—"Lad, my cousin says you are a promising young surveyor and an upright youth. I may have use for your services."

Lord Fairfax was as good as his word. Before mid-March George was invited to go with Colonel

Fairfax's son on an expedition to survey some of those western lands. What an opportunity! At last George was going into the wilderness to see with his own eyes what lay on the other side of the mountains.

His companion George William Fairfax was twenty-three. They were the best of friends, but George respectfully called the older youth "Mr. Fairfax." For George William was a justice of the County Court and a member of the Virginia House of Burgesses.

Traveling light, the pair covered forty miles on horseback the first day, then joined the surveyor James Genn, who was to be in charge. When the party crossed the crest of the Blue Ridge, George Washington looked out on a wider world than he had ever seen before. Before him lay the beautiful valley of the Shenandoah. Far off to the northwest even higher mountains towered.

Along the western riverbank of this green plain the men looked at the site of Lord Fairfax's future home. The soil was richer than any George had seen before. This land would surely be valuable someday. Farther down the valley they put up in a frontier cabin and hired their working force. Here George really learned about doing without the comforts of home. The men lay on the floor in their clothes to sleep. But George heard there was a bed in the next room, so he stripped and prepared himself to rest more elegantly.

To George's surprise, the "bed" was only a bit of matted straw. He crept under the threadbare blanket, for it was chilly in the hills. To make matters worse, the blanket was full of fleas and bedbugs! Scratching and shivering, poor George waited until the light was out in the other room. Then he slipped into his clothes and lay down quietly beside his companions.

He was glad they didn't hear him. What a greenhorn they would think he was!

After that, George didn't look for beds in the wilderness. The choice berth, he discovered, was the spot on the floor nearest the fireplace. Soon he thought it even better to sleep outdoors.

As the men headed toward the south branch of the Potomac in the high Alleghenies, they plunged into real Indian country. Floods, fed by heavy March rains, swelled the rivers. Mr. Genn had some of the men unload the horses and swim them across the torrents. Others in canoes brought over the supplies. The trail was overgrown with grass and weeds and blocked by fallen trees.

Harder and harder the spring rains beat down. But finally the expedition reached the south branch at Cresap's Camp. This was a point on the Indian warrior path. Here the party holed in to sit out the storm.

On the third day it cleared at noon and the sun came out. That afternoon George saw a winding line of bronze figures slipping silently down the forest path under the dripping trees. Soon thirty young braves in war paint were at the camp—the first wild Indians George had ever seen.

A man at the camp who spoke their tongue learned they were a war party returning from battle. A little sheepishly they displayed a single bloody scalp. They were ashamed of so small a catch.

Genn's men persuaded the redskins to put on a war dance. George made careful notes of all he saw. Here was something to tell about when he got home!

One of the Indians borrowed a pot, filled it half full of water, then stretched deerskin over the top. This was a drum. Another had a gourd filled with shot and decorated with a horse's tail. It rattled when he shook it, the tail fluttering in the air.

The warriors cleared a large circle. They gathered wood and a roaring fire was soon going, though the ground was damp. The redskins huddled around it.

A leader now spoke to the dancers, telling them with grunts and signs what to do. One of the band got up as if from sleep, then leaped into the circle and began to weave about the flames. To the accompaniment of drum and gourd, other warriors followed. Shadows played on the sleek brown bodies.

The surveyors spent all next day with the Indians

and then were off still farther upstream. On Patterson Creek they were the guests of a frontier judge. He was an officer of the King and set a good table, but it had no cloth—and they ate with their jackknives.

Finally the crew went to work marking out boundaries in the forest. It was a great day for George when he ran his own survey lines for the first time. In his field notes he neatly entered the landmarks, such as "a black walnut and a locust" or "a large hickory struck by lightning."

George and his companions camped wherever the end of the day's work found them. Once the tent caught fire. A couple of times strong winds blew it down on their heads. George spent a month in the wilderness. He saw many new things. He learned to make his bed where he found it and to cook his own food over an open fire. He even learned to endure the pangs of hunger.

He had seen a war dance of the redskins, fresh from a scalping party.

Why, after this George could meet almost any situation that might arise! And now the mission was over. Young Fairfax and young Washington set off over the hills for the lower Potomac. In the Blue Ridge, the day before they reached home, one more adventure was to come. They encountered a rattle-snake—or, as George wrote, a "rattled snake."

The two youths had seen just about everything.

Chapter 4: HEIR OF LAWRENCE

HEADING THE LIST of things he would need on his trip, George wrote in a bold hand, "my Razor." He added waistcoats, shirts, collars, neckcloths—and caps to keep his hair in place after he had dressed and powdered it. Summer had come in Virginia. Thick leaves and tall grass cut off the view. Until fall the young surveyor would find it hard to mark off land.

So with a party of spirited friends he visited gay Yorktown on the coast. They would dine well and enjoy whatever fashionable events were at hand. These might be a full-dress ball, a cockfight, even a play by a troupe of actors from England.

George now wanted to appear to good advantage wherever he went. He cut a fine figure in satin and broadcloth. In homes where he was a guest, George learned billiards and whist. If only he could be at ease in the company of young ladies! Somehow they didn't seem to be as interested in him as he was in them. This worried George, for he was not ready to shut women out of his life.

Young Washington was not easily discouraged when he set his mind to something. Hadn't he become a surveyor by learning all he could from books before taking to the field? Searching through the Mount Vernon library, he found that a great deal had been written about women, too. Much of it was in verse. Poets told of wounds they had suffered from Cupid's darts. They begged their ladies to take pity on them.

It was for a certain Frances Alexander that George's heart was heavy. So he tried his hand at an acrostic. Each line began with a letter of her name. Four lines before the end, however, George ran out of nice things to say about Frances.

How envious George was when, at Christmas time, young Fairfax married the lovely Sally Cary. She was a gay lass of eighteen and a gifted hostess, whose lively parties added to the merriment of the neighborhood. Sally Fairfax had a rare gift of getting shy people to talk. She made George feel that everything he said was well worth listening to.

"If only other young women were like Sally!" George sighed.

Well, Sally had a sister named Mary. He began to look forward to Mary's visits.

Among the cultured Fairfaxes there was much talk of books and plays. This led George to learn more of English history and read Addison's essays. A play by Addison, *The Tragedy of Cato*, was a favorite in the amateur dramatics that filled long winter evenings at Belvoir. Cato was shown as a brave general of the last days of the Roman Republic before Caesar made himself Emperor. Speaking out with a fiery tongue and a fearless heart, Cato tried to save the old Roman liberties:

Remember, O my friends, the laws, the rights,
The gen'rous plan of power delivered down,
From age to age, by your renowned forefathers,
(So dearly bought, the price of so much blood)
O let it never perish in your hands!

Although the sad story was laid in Rome, it was written by an Englishman to protect English freedoms. Acting parts in the play, George learned his lines well. He never forgot them. As long as George Washington lived, Cato's stirring words stayed alive inside him, along with memories of happy evenings at Belvoir.

All they could talk about at Mount Vernon around George's seventeenth birthday was the big land grant to the Ohio Company. Imagine, half a million acres! This wild land beyond the Alleghenies must be claimed by Englishmen before the French moved in from Canada and the Great Lakes. So a fort and an Indian trading post were to be established. The company would get settlers to make their homes out there. Lawrence and Austin Washington had a part in this plan.

Closer at home they were founding a new city on the Potomac. It was called Alexandria. George helped with the survey and drew the town map. Mount Vernon was more his home nowadays than Ferry Farm.

In another four years, by his father's will, George would own the plantation where his mother lived. Augustine Washington had made arrangements for his widow's support. Nevertheless, she was tortured by fears of being poor. She poured her worries into George's ears when he came to the Rappahannock.

Poor lady! She had been orphaned as a girl. Now, all too young, she was a widow with no one to look to for protection except George. Already he knew in his heart he could never ask her to move.

"There is no lack of land in the West," he told himself. "I will carve out my own plantation."

So now George tried harder than ever to make

money. That summer he became surveyor for Culpeper County. And in the fall Lord Fairfax called him to the Shenandoah country to measure off more of his great holdings. The youth worked long after cold weather set in. At night he rolled up in a bearskin rug.

George couldn't get to Belvoir as often as before, though he did meet Sally's sister Mary Cary. By this time, though, he was more interested in Betsy Fauntleroy. Anyway, love would have to wait. A man needed property before he could think of marrying.

October 16, 1750, was a red-letter day. Since the price was right, George bought 453 acres of fertile Shenandoah land. Nine days later he got another 550 acres from Lord Fairfax. Before the year was out he made a down payment on a third tract, this time of 456 acres.

So now George was owner of 1,459 acres of good land beyond the Blue Ridge. Not bad for a youth of eighteen who had earned it all by his own toil!

The land lay on a fork of Bullskin Creek just before it flows into the Shenandoah.

"I shall call it my Bullskin plantation," said the young landowner with excusable pride.

Lawrence Washington was becoming a big figure in the colony. Even Governor Dinwiddie now joined with him in the Ohio Company.

Many Germans were eager to settle on the western lands, but they had their own religious beliefs and did not want to pay taxes to the official church as other Virginians did. Lawrence became a champion of religious liberty, saying they should not be made to pay this tax. North Carolina and Pennsylvania, he pointed out, were becoming prosperous because they welcomed newcomers of many creeds.

Lawrence's health had been bad ever since he came back from the war. Now, with all his new work, he lost more weight and had severe coughing spells. Three daughters had been born to Lawrence and Anne, but all had died as babies. Now they had a fourth child, also a girl. How much Lawrence wanted a son—to be his heir and carry on the family name! So far this had been denied him. Suppose his health grew no better. . . .

Perhaps some dark fear now drew him even closer to George in brotherly affection. Toward the end of 1751 Lawrence was warned not to pass another winter in Virginia. By now it was clear that he was suffering from tuberculosis. The doctor believed a warm climate might do him good. Lawrence decided to go to Barbados Island in the West Indies. He could not take his wife and baby into the tropics. So he asked George to join him.

It was the first time George had been to sea. From being at the wharf, though, he could recognize ships of every cut and rig. During the voyage of five weeks he learned the name of every rope and spar. He fished for shark and dolphin in the bright blue waters and kept a log of storms and passing vessels.

It was exciting early one morning to hear the cry, "Land, land!" and know that they had arrived.

Though it was November, the tropical island was a brilliant green. There were limes, pineapples and fruits George had never seen before.

Major Clarke, a relative of the Fairfaxes, made the Washingtons welcome and helped them find lodgings. Even though there was smallpox in his family, he insisted they dine with him.

"Maybe we shouldn't go," George whispered as Major Clarke was leaving.

"Hush!" said Lawrence. "A Virginia gentleman never offends a gracious host."

During the next couple of weeks these courteous Virginians were entertained in many homes. They went to the theater, looked at the fortifications and visited sugar plantations. George made notes on the guns of Fort James and the profit to be made from sugar.

Suddenly sight-seeing was interrupted. George awoke with a burning fever and an aching head. Red spots were breaking out on his face two days later. The doctor said, yes, George had smallpox.

For three weeks the youth bore the pain and itching manfully. After he was up, the mirror showed him the scars and pits he would carry on his face for life. He was glad the disfigurement was no worse.

It was his brother's trouble that caused him real worry. Lawrence grew no better. He tired of the never-ending heat in Barbados and decided to try the milder climate of Bermuda. He sent George home to see if his wife and child could join him there.

"When you reach Virginia, stop in Williamsburg and give this letter to Governor Dinwiddie," he said. "A young man in your position should be acquainted in the capital."

So, on his return, George dined with the governor. He would have enjoyed it more could he have stopped thinking of Lawrence's drawn face.

Lawrence went to Bermuda. Before Anne could make her plans, however, he grew very ill and came home to Virginia to die. Just before the end came, Lawrence called George to his bedside.

"I shall never have a son," he said. "My infant daughter I leave to your guardianship. Carry on in my place. I know you will do honor to our name."

Chapter 5: MESSENGER TO THE FRENCH

JUST BEFORE his twenty-first birthday George became Major Washington. Following in Lawrence's footsteps, he now commanded the militia. The light in the study at Mount Vernon glimmered late. George was studying war.

Soon he was full master at Mount Vernon. Lawrence's little daughter, like her sisters before her, did not live. George arranged to buy the widow's interest in the property.

He was a bachelor still and seemed likely to remain one. Betsy Fauntleroy had turned him down. And it was too late to woo Sally Fairfax's charming sister Mary, for now her heart belonged to another.

There was important work to be done in any case, the young major realized, as he stood before Governor Dinwiddie getting his orders. It was the end of October in 1753. There was a tang in the air.

The portly man in the big white wig spoke gravely. "Do not forget for a moment, Major Washington, that this is a mission of great trust. You have been chosen to carry out the wishes of our King and place this message in the hands of the French commander."

The letter, George knew, demanded that the French leave His Majesty's lands on the Ohio at once. The governor continued. "You are to await a reply and you are to learn all you can of the plans of the French and their strength. Make haste, for there is not a day to be lost."

Major Washington took the paper bearing the King's seal. "I shall be off this very day, Your Honor," he said.

On the way to Fredericksburg George made his plans. The journey would take him farther to the north and deeper into the wild country than he had ever been. Winter was setting in. Supplies, blankets and warm clothing were necessary.

George was to hold a council with the friendly Indians and make sure they would stand with the English against the French. Both countries had their eyes on the Ohio. They were lining up the tribes for the coming struggle. So George made a note to take along plenty of presents to gain Indian friendships.

At Fredericksburg he looked up the fencing master Jacob van Braam, who spoke French and went along as interpreter. Horses were bought and loaded at Winchester.

They crossed into Maryland at Wills Creek. Here the Ohio Company agent Christopher Gist joined the party. Only the Indians knew the western woods as well as this shrewd frontiersman. With Gist's marksmanship and sense of direction they would not lack for game or lose their way.

The party moved on to territory now part of Pennsylvania. They forded swollen rivers, pushed through laurel thickets and climbed into the mountain snows. It was bleak country, but there was venison to eat because Gist's rifle always found its mark.

At the mouth of Turtle Creek the men reached John Frazier's store. This old Indian trader had news aplenty. The French had driven him from his trading post at Venango, vowing they would allow no English traders in this western land. Worse yet, they had roused three Indian nations to take up the hatchet against the British.

Indians on the warpath! Major Washington knew this was bad medicine, indeed. He would have to talk well to hold the remaining Indians on the English side.

What a sight! For a long time George gazed upon the two rivers coming together. The sluggish Monongahela, deep and still . . . the Allegheny, hurrying head-on from the north to this meeting place . . . the forested bottom land in the triangle just before these rivers joined to form the mighty Ohio.

The Golden Triangle it would one day be called—in the heart of Pittsburgh. George did not know this, of course. But he saw the spot—overlooking both rivers—as just the place for a fort. Here was the place to beat the French to the draw before they took over the Ohio Valley.

The party got across the foaming Allegheny and went downstream to Logstown. This was a cluster of Indian huts—with a long house where Half King and his fellow chieftains met in council.

It was Half King, the great Seneca and good friend of the English, with whom the young major had business. Among the Six Nations of the Iroquois no man might call himself fully a king, but Half King was a real power. Bearing presents of tobacco and beads, Washington waited on the Indian leader. The grave Half King, a man past fifty but straight as a forest tree, welcomed the major. With sudden fierce gestures he told how the French had killed his father. The French commander had heaped on insult by telling the proud redskin:

"I am not afraid of flies or mosquitoes or Indians.

Child, you talk foolish. You say this land belongs to you. Not even the black under my nails is yours!"

Now, with his English friends by his side, Half King swore to take revenge on the French. He sent into the forests and called a council. Major Washington studied his words well before entering the long house. He would speak through an interpreter. Even so, much would depend on his speech.

"Your brother, the governor of Virginia," said Washington, "wants me to ask you for some of your young men. He wants them to provide supplies for us on our way and be a guard against the French Indians who have taken up the hatchet against us."

How could the Indians refuse this request and not seem like cowards?

Half King promised the young major all he asked for. "You may depend on it that we will be your guide," he said. He promised also to make a speech of defiance to the French and give them back their wampum belts. The Indians' return of these treaty belts would be a sign that now they were enemies.

George was pleased with the success of this, his first council. Before long, he found he had taken too much for granted. There were four days of delay in getting off. George fumed and fretted. But there was no way to hurry up the Indians. Some of the tribes were not ready to fling their treaty belts at the feet of the French. Why should they make enemies until they knew how much help the English really meant to give?

So young Washington had only a redskin guard of four—two minor chieftains and a young hunter, besides the loyal Half King.

December was now at hand. The men moved north into freezing rains. The place they stopped at the first night was called Murdering Town. But Washington was glad to be on his way.

On December 4th the Virginians and the Indians came to the log building from which trader Frazier had been driven. Over it flew the flag of France, boldly defying the claim of England to this soil. They had reached Venango. It was now the duty of the young soldier to warn the intruders to leave.

Instead of the rude reception the party had expected, the French welcomed Washington and his companions with much show of hospitality. Captain Joncaire could not do enough to make them comfortable. He was as polite to the Indians as to the white men and spoke to them in their own tongue—for his mother was a Seneca and he was half Indian himself.

By now, the foolish commander who had offended Half King was dead. Fine fare was placed before the Indians. Joncaire would not think of taking back the treaty belt from his Indian friends.

Neither would he take the letter from the governor

of Virginia. The real French commander, he told Major Washington, was at Fort Le Boeuf. This meant they would have to journey north for five days. But the French would provide an escort.

At dinner, a French officer boasted that soon they would seize the entire Ohio Valley.

"True, you English settlers outnumber us two to one. But you will not know how to move as quickly as we can," he said.

George had to bite his tongue and think hard about his rules of civility and decent behavior. How provoking these Frenchmen were—to talk of taking the very lands to which Lawrence had given the last strength of his short life!

The winds were howling, the rains descending and the creeks overflowing on the path between Venango and Fort Le Boeuf. A quieter drama was going on within the strangely mixed group. The smooth French were trying all the while to woo the Indians away.

Matters got even worse at Fort Le Boeuf. St. Pierre, the commanding officer, was an old man with only one eye but as clever as a fox. Beside him, Half King, for all his Indian wiles, was a simple soul. St. Pierre was free with fine promises and gifts of firearms.

This spot was almost at Lake Erie. The French commander urged Washington to go on to Canada and take his message to the French governor there. But the major would go no farther. He insisted on a reply. St. Pierre left no doubt what it would be.

"The country belongs to us," he told Washington. "No Englishman has a right to trade here—and I have orders to arrest any who try."

While they waited the Virginians kept their eyes and ears open to study the fort. It was a stockade of blockhouses and sharp-pointed poles. Cannon were mounted at each corner. And on the creek were more than two hundred canoes, with still others being built. There was no doubt what this meant. The French were planning to move south in the spring . . . south into the lands of the Ohio.

All George wanted now was to get his answer and hurry back to Williamsburg to warn Governor Din-widdie. Finally they set off in canoes down the river, while others of the party went with the horses to join them at Venango. By Christmas Eve the weakened horses were stumbling in the snow. The men were frostbitten. Washington had to turn the horses over to Van Braam, while he and Gist set off on foot over frozen fields with packs and guns. It was the only way to get the message to Williamsburg in time.

George, used to the saddle, became footsore the second day. But they pushed on. Beyond Murdering Town they fell in with a strange Indian who insisted on being their guide. Deep in the woods the redskin

47

wheeled suddenly and fired on the pair. He missed—
and Gist and Washington grappled with him. George
wouldn't let the Indian be killed. So they sent him
away and traveled all night. They were afraid the
strange Indian would return, looking for their scalps.

They planned to cross the Allegheny on the ice.
Instead they found open water in the middle with
cakes of ice crashing down the dangerous course.

Gist and Washington cut trees and built a raft.
Since they had but one hatchet between them, however, it took all day. They tried to pole the raft between the cakes of ice. But soon they were locked in
an ice jam. While steadying the raft, George was
pitched into the water. He struggled back on board.
The men had to spend the night on a small island, their
clothing stiff with ice.

After hours of misery, the dawn brought hope to
the shivering men. The river now was frozen over
solidly and they walked to the other bank. Soon they
were back in Frazier's trading post, where warm
clothing and fresh horses were to be had.

By the new year, Washington was crossing the
mountains again on his way to Williamsburg with the
French reply. On January 16th the young major
placed the precious message in the hands of Governor
Dinwiddie. It had been guarded well, deep inside his
pack, during the dangerous journey. The writing was
clear and the paper dry.

Chapter 6: TOO LITTLE, TOO LATE

TIRED from the long journey, young Major Washington rubbed his eyes and braced himself to stay awake all night. He was preparing the notes of his exciting trip. The printer must have them by morning.

Governor Dinwiddie had said: "The people of the colonies have their eyes shut to the French danger. We must let them know what you have seen."

What Washington had seen was neatly entered in his exercise book. It was not intended for the eyes of others. The young officer had never been to school in England. He knew he was weak in spelling and grammar.

But orders were orders. George was a good soldier. He corrected his notes the best he could. Soon they were being read in all the colonies and even in London.

The governor ordered a fort built at the meeting place of the rivers, where George had stood. Now there must be soldiers to guard the carpenters.

The burgesses voted ten thousand pounds for defense—but on one condition. Fourteen of their own members were to watch over the spending. The money, they felt, was Virginia money. The royal governor was furious. He called this a "republican way of thinking" and an insult to the King. But he had to give in, because the French were coming.

Dinwiddie sent messengers galloping south to the Carolinas and north to Pennsylvania and New York. Send us help to drive the French out of the Ohio Valley, he begged.

Washington went out to enlist troops. Hardly anyone, though, wanted to leave home and face the French and Indians in the wilderness. So the governor said that each volunteer should have fifteen pounds of tobacco a day—and free land besides. With this promise, Washington recruited a hundred men.

He did not have a high opinion of his troops. They were loose and idle fellows, slow to mind. Some were without shoes and shirts. Uniforms were hard to get. With his new duties, Washington became a lieutenant colonel. He was not very happy about it, though, for as a colonial he earned only half as much pay as a British officer.

Virginia was ill prepared to resist the French. But there was no time to be lost. Governor Dinwiddie ordered Washington to march west and do his best.

"You are to act on the defensive, if possible, but we must protect the building of the fort," he said. More troops would follow under the experienced Colonel Joshua Fry—and surely there would be help from the other colonies. But passing weeks brought only excuses and delay. The colonies were not used to working together. Why should they put themselves out to defend Virginia soil?

Washington reached Winchester—and there he found out that wagons were not to be had for love or money. He raged at the Shenandoah settlers. If the French were not defeated, he warned, soon they would turn loose their Indians to raid this very countryside. But the farmers did not want to give up their wagons. By force of law, Washington finally seized ten teams, paying well for them. The grumbling owners took care to surrender their lamest nags and their most broken-down vehicles.

Precious days were passing. The horses were so weak going uphill that the soldiers had to get behind the wagons and push. The ragged men grew tired and dropped dark hints of desertion.

Washington rode ahead to pick camp sites and find river crossings. One day he met a messenger hurrying from the half-built fort beyond the mountain.

Eight hundred French were coming! An attack was expected at any hour. Washington relayed this news to Colonel Fry, begging for help.

The forlorn column dragged into Wills Creek, Maryland, a few days later. Beyond this point not even wagons could move on the miserable road— only pack horses. And the horses Washington had been promised from the Ohio country were not there! Instead came more gloomy news.

The French had captured the site of the fort. They had driven away the carpenters at gun point.

What the English had begun, the French took over. The place where the Ohio River starts they now named Fort Duquesne. No one was more unhappy over this than Half King. He had laid the first log of the English fort, proud to defy his father's slayers. And now the French had the fort and were at his doorstep. The chief sent a runner to Washington.

"If you do not come to our assistance now, I think we shall never meet together again." These were Half King's mournful words.

The lieutenant colonel did not dare let his Indian ally know how weak he was. He replied that he was cutting a road through the forest. Over it the King's many warriors would soon advance. "Our hearts burn with love toward you," he wrote, and signed himself "Your Friend and Brother, George Washington Conotocarious." This last was a name the redskins had given him—and meant one who is very fierce and destroys villages.

The road of which he told Half King would lead over the mountains to the Monongahela. There he hoped to dig in until guns could move down the river and attack Fort Duquesne.

All the while young Washington couldn't help feeling put out. So little help came from Virginia. When it did, it was late. Most of all, Washington needed presents to hold the friendship of the Indians. Even to get a guide he had to give away one of his own ruffled shirts. This he couldn't afford to do, he was traveling so light.

Governor Dinwiddie was irked by these complaints. He wrote Washington that there are always hardships in a soldier's life and he should look on them as opportunities for glory. The lieutenant colonel's pride was stung at this. He replied, "I am hardy enough to undergo the most severe trials."

Late in May the little army reached the Great Meadows. Washington wrote it down as "a charming field for an encounter." He set men to clearing the bushes. Others went out to scout the enemy, for the Indians told of seeing strange footprints.

In this there was more than rumor. The frontiersman Gist came to tell how fifty Frenchmen had
threatened to destroy his settlement. A messenger
from Half King had news of prowling Frenchmen.
Washington set out at the head of a group of men to
meet his Indian friend. It was a pitch-black and rainy
night. They lost the trail and struggled through wet
bushes, their bodies drenched. At dawn they met
Half King and a dozen of his men. The Indian leader
sent scouts to follow the enemy trail. They returned,
having located the French hide-out in the woods.

Virginians and redskins now went out to encircle
the French. At eight in the morning of May 28th they
closed in on them, Washington's men in front, the
Indians in the rear. The position most open to fire
was on the right. Washington led that himself.

There was a hush before the tall figure stepped into
the open and gave the command to attack. The
French, surprised, reached for their rifles. Shots rang
out. Washington heard bullets whistle past his ear.

Who fired first? It happened so quickly that no one
knew. But it was the shot that started the French and
Indian War . . . a war that was to last seven years.

Men were dropping. Washington's force closed in.
The French fell back. Then, seeing Indians behind
them, they threw up their hands and came toward
the Virginians. They had no wish to be scalped.

In fifteen minutes the battle was over. Ten Frenchmen and one Virginian were dead. A bullet from Half King's gun had taken the life of Jumonville, the French commander. Some of the wounded were tomahawked, but Washington was able to protect the lives of twenty-one prisoners. One Frenchman escaped to carry the news to Fort Duquesne.

Next morning Lieutenant Colonel Washington sent his prisoners, with a guard, to Governor Dinwiddie. The French complained of this, saying they came in peace and not in war. They claimed they were merely bearers of a warning, like Washington the winter before. This did not make sense to Washington. If it were so, he asked, why did they come in such numbers and so secretly?

George knew the French would not take this defeat lying down. He hoped Colonel Fry and his men would soon arrive. Meanwhile, the young commander began building a rough sort of fort on the Great Meadows. Without more supplies and men he did not dare go ahead too far.

On June 6th the cook complained that the flour had given out. And every day there were more mouths to feed. Squaws and hungry Indian children were taking shelter at the English camp. Their braves, having dared the anger of the French, felt they had a right to send them there for protection.

The same day brought word that Colonel Fry was

dead . . . killed in a fall from his horse as he was hurrying west to join the expedition. So now Washington was made a full colonel and put in command of the war against the French. He had not wanted so much responsibility. But there was no choice.

Help arrived from South Carolina a week later. Colonel Washington went out to welcome a company of soldiers and their leader, Captain Mackay.

The high-toned captain was spick and span. He made it clear at once that he was a captain by the King's commission. This made him a British officer. He wouldn't think of taking orders from a colonial, even a colonel.

This was no time to lose one's temper, but Washington was really annoyed. Here they were, way out in the wilderness, expecting an attack at any hour. How could there be two commanders giving orders?

Then the Indians grew restless. So few gifts, so little food, so many Frenchmen! They were very unhappy about it all, they told the colonel.

Next came a message from Chief Monakatoocha that the French were making ready to march against Washington with twelve hundred men. Washington called the officers together. All that could be done, they decided, was to dig in on the Great Meadows and hope that help from Virginia might arrive in time.

It was a case of necessity. So Washington named

the place Fort Necessity. It was a poor spot for a battle, he now recognized. High wooded ground on two sides offered cover to an enemy. The Indians did not think much of it either. Silently, one by one, they slipped away. Finally even Half King left.

The defenders dug trenches and hastily built a stockade. They were wet and tired. It was raining the morning of July 3rd when a sentinel fired a shot.

Colonel Washington saw three columns of French attackers approaching. He ordered his men into the trenches. Wallowing in water they loaded their muskets. The first volley was from the enemy, still some distance away.

"Withhold your fire until you can take good aim," said Washington coolly. They had no ammunition to waste.

The French drew nearer. First they took care to kill the horses and cows. Soon Washington had no pack animals or beef cattle left. Then from behind trees they began picking off his men. Yet all that rainy afternoon the Virginians and the Carolinians held off the attackers. If a Frenchman stuck his head out for just a moment, a bullet whizzed his way.

But Washington was hopelessly outnumbered. By evening a quarter of his men were dead or wounded. Then came a mighty cloudburst. The guns were fouled, the ammunition was waterlogged. The fort itself was almost a pond.

"Will you parley?" cried a French officer at eight o'clock.

Washington refused to meet with them. He feared a trick to get spies into his pitiful shelter. Then the French asked for someone able to speak their language, promising his safe return. The colonel chose his interpreter Van Braam.

Generous terms of surrender were offered. Washington's force might depart with military honors. All they had to do was leave two hostages behind. This was to guarantee the return of the French prisoners in Virginia. With this the French would be satisfied.

Surrender papers were drawn up in the rainstorm and translated to Washington by the light of a guttering candle. There was nothing to do but sign.

A new day was dawning. It was July 4th. Washington rounded up his survivors. He made sure the wounded were cared for. He destroyed all the supplies except those his soldiers could carry on their backs, for he had no horses left.

At 10:00 A.M. the mud-spattered men marched out of Fort Necessity with colors flying and a brave drumbeat. They set out on the long march home.

Colonel Washington was leaving with honor but his heart was heavy. It carried the weight of knowing that not all that goes with war is glory.

Chapter 7: REDCOATS AND BUCKSKINS

THE FORT NECESSITY defeat put Governor Dinwiddie in a blaming mood. He blamed the contractors
for failing to deliver goods in time. He blamed
the other colonies because fighting men were all
too few to whip the French. He declared that the
only way to treat the lazy, good-for-nothing colonists in America was to lay a tax on them by act of
Parliament. Then you could pay a British army to
clean up the mess at Fort Duquesne.

In fact, the fretful Dinwiddie blamed everyone but
himself. He even blamed Washington, saying that
with so few men he should not have gone so far. But

most of George's neighbors were proud of him. The burgesses passed a resolution praising his "gallant and brave behavior in defense of his country."

People were even ready to overlook the trick the French played on him in those surrender papers. Of course, George didn't know a word of French. But there was his name, as big as life, to a confession that his party had assassinated Jumonville in time of peace. It was part of the same French claim that they were only coming with a warning when the first shots had rung out.

Washington and his fellow officers knew of no such "confession." They said the translator Van Braam must have skipped over that part—or maybe he didn't see it in the heavy rain. The Dutchman, whose native tongue was neither French nor English, was not there to speak for himself. He was one of the two hostages left behind.

Then the pride of the high-spirited young officer received another blow . . . a blow he would not take this time. Dinwiddie decided that no colonial officer was to hold a rank higher than captain. So Colonel Washington gave up his military title and became plain Mr. Washington. Rather than suffer such unfairness he would raise tobacco.

In England, all this while, a big plan to smash the French was shaping up. This time the attacking force would be under British command. It would hit the enemy all along the line. While General Braddock was taking back Fort Duquesne, armies in the North would march against Niagara and Lake Champlain.

It was a proud day for the new town of Alexandria when the great Braddock landed. He had forty years of British army training behind him. Young Washington watched Braddock's red-coated troops step from the boats and march in perfect order, every man in step. They made a handsome sight with buttons polished and guns gleaming.

How fine these well-drilled regiments looked— beside Washington's raggle-taggle force! Where he had found it uphill work to enlist a few score men, Virginians could hardly wait to enter Braddock's army. George ate his heart out wanting to go along. But he was too proud to take a lowered rank.

The great families of the Northern Neck entertained Braddock and his gallant officers. Around the banquet table the general must have heard much praise of the fearless young Washington, who knew the western country so well. Perhaps it was the gay Sally Fairfax who whispered in the gruff commander's ear how brave Washington was and yet how sensitive.

One day a message came to Mount Vernon from Braddock's headquarters. Washington was invited to join the general's military "family." Here there would be no question of rank. He would take orders from no one but the great General Braddock himself.

The young man's heart bounded. So, after all, he was to have a part in driving the French from Fort Duquesne. What's more, he would study the art of war under a famous British commander. In May, 1755, George Washington reported to General Braddock and was named his aide-de-camp.

General Braddock liked Washington at once. This was remarkable, for very little else in America pleased him. His hot temper flared up when supplies failed to come or were unfit to use. When meat smelled so bad it had to be buried, Braddock stormed that the colonists were people "without honor or honesty, capable of nothing but lies and villainy."

Only one colonial besides Washington seemed to be in his good books. This was Benjamin Franklin of Philadelphia, who rounded up one hundred and fifty wagons and delivered them on time. Yet this was only after one of Braddock's angry officers had threatened to take them by force—and burn the settlers' homes in the bargain. How different this country was from Europe, where an army was feared and obeyed!

And what blistering letters Braddock sent London about these stubborn Americans!

Neither did he have much use for the Virginia troops in his command. They seemed to have no spirit. A shining exception, in Braddock's eyes, was the tall young Washington—cocky at times, but ready for any duty and firm and level in his gaze. Braddock permitted Washington to say things for which he would have silenced others.

At table, the words grew hot as the old general and the twenty-three-year-old beginner argued about traveling light and fast and using Indian tactics in this wild country. The red-faced Braddock lashed out at Washington for his impertinence. A moment later, though, he had to smile at the sight of this bold cub giving lessons to an old soldier who knew the famous battlefields of Europe.

During the march over the mountains Washington complained that Braddock paused to level every molehill and bridge every creek. While the young man wore Indian dress, the regular troops sweltered in red coats and stiff uniforms. Proud of their soldiers' finery, they had a term of scorn for the colonials. "Buckskins" they called them.

To pay the British back, the Americans sat around the campfire telling tall tales about the Indians. Soon the redcoats were ready to jump if so much as a twig snapped in the dark woods. The buckskins even worked themselves into a scare!

Just when the goal seemed at last in sight, Washington was seized by a violent fever. The general made him lie in a rear camp for several days. The aide consented only on the promise that he would be allowed to ride forward in time for the battle.

On the eve of battle Washington was so weak that he had to fix cushions into his saddle to ride at all. But he was up at 2:00 A.M. on July 9th, delivering Braddock's orders. He was getting heavy wagons and artillery across the Monongahela, hoping it would be done before the French attacked them there.

More anxious moments came as the sun rode high and they crossed the river a second time. Everyone breathed more easily after that. Now they were within striking distance of Fort Duquesne, only a few miles away. Surely if the French were going to attack they would have done so by now.

Riding with Braddock, Washington could see the mile-long column through the sparsely wooded country ahead. It was a proud army, fifteen hundred strong. Men in red and mounted guns were moving forward in perfect order, flanked by light horse (a branch of cavalry in those days) and grenadiers.

The head of the column was out of sight when firing was heard in midafternoon. The sound grew louder. Volley after volley rang out. Braddock, with Washington at his side, went racing to the front.

When they got there they were astounded, so great was the confusion. Broken ranks of men were huddled in a pocket. The head of the column was crushing back in panic on the men behind. Those who kept their heads were busy loading and shooting, but they aimed at an unseen foe. Upon them poured a deadly fire, coming from nowhere, unless from behind rocks and trees and clumps of brush. But though no face was seen, bloodcurdling war whoops rose at times.

Braddock could not believe his eyes and ears. An officer dashed up begging him to storm the hill on the north, then collapsed from his wounds. Others were trying to rescue artillery that lay on lower ground to the south, between road and river. A third direction, the road leading west, was under fire as well.

How could all this have happened? There was no time to ask now. What had to be done at all costs was to take the hill and get back the big guns. Washington sped Braddock's commands to the officers.

Dazed redcoats were shooting their own comrades. One of the Virginia officers led a charge on the hill. He lost most of his men because they were mistaken for French.

From time to time a half-naked redskin dashed into the open a moment, yelling and brandishing a knife. He took a scalp, then darted back and became invisible.

Buckskins along the eastern flank took cover behind trees and fought in the Indian manner. Redcoated officers galloped about trying to restore some discipline, if only to retreat in order. Their mounted figures formed an easy target. Most of them were killed or wounded.

As long as the battle lasted, the tall form of Washington was in the thick of it. Bullets ripped into his hat and slit his uniform in several places. Two horses were shot from under him. He mounted a third, still unhurt.

Braddock himself was not so lucky. Like Washington he lost two horses, but then a bullet pierced his lung. He lay helpless on the ground.

With the officers gone, there was no holding the frightened men. Wagoners cut the horses loose and made off as fast as they could go. Soldiers stampeded behind them, throwing away their guns . . . "breaking and running like sheep pursued by dogs," Washington was later to say.

The rout was complete. A few hundred French and Indians, fighting from behind trees, had defeated a British army of three times their number.

Few remained behind to help their general on that sad flight. Washington lifted the wounded Braddock into a cart and ordered him carried to the rear. The general, though in great pain, talked of rallying his soldiers. Even now they outnumbered the enemy.

It had been the luck of the French to fan out and surround the head of the British column in a place that formed a natural trap. Try again—and it might be England's turn for luck. But there was no getting anyone to listen to reason any more.

So General Braddock sent Washington on a long

journey to the rear for supplies and help. The young aide had climbed from a sickbed to the saddle for that dreadful day. Now he rode all night, his horse stumbling in darkness over wounded men. They had crawled that far and were dying. There was not even time to stop and help them. Next day Washington was back helping with the retreat. The general himself was dying now.

"Who would have thought it?" Braddock mumbled. "We shall know how to deal with them better another time."

Near the Great Meadows, where Washington had met his defeat the year before, the general breathed his last, grateful that his aide was at his side.

Washington read the service of the Church over the body of the brave soldier. They buried Braddock in the center of the road. Army wagons rolled over the spot to hide the grave from scalp-hunting enemies.

Some of these redskins had fired many times at Washington while the battle raged. No wonder a legend took root that he was under the protection of spirits. Years later an aged Indian repeated this legend. What he said of Washington went like this:

"He is not of the redcoat tribe. He has Indian wisdom—and his warriors fight as we do. He will never die in battle but will become a chief of nations."

Chapter 8: PATIENCE AND REWARD

MAYBE MRS. MARY WASHINGTON hadn't heard the Indian legend. Anyway, she put little stock in the idea that a bullet couldn't hurt her son. She begged him, as she had many times before, to give up fighting for something safer. Right now, George was half ready to listen to her advice, his disappointments had been so many. He had lost money. His health was bad. The English soldiers had called him a buckskin. Now he had seen their "dastardly behavior."

With Braddock dead, the redcoats pulled back all the way to Philadelphia. They left the frontier open to Indian attack. It was this grave danger that finally

68

forced Washington to become a soldier again. The colony had to protect itself. No other Virginian had Washington's military experience.

"It is your duty to take the command and organize our defenses," the leading burgesses told him.

So, in September, 1755, Washington became Virginia's commander-in-chief.

Indian raids were starting when he reached Winchester. Settlers fled from their homes and crowded into the valley town for safety. Washington toured the little forts on the western rivers. He rode through fields of ripe corn left unharvested.

Fortunately, winter was close. The warrior paths from the Ohio would soon be blocked by snow. This gave the commander time to prepare his officers for the hard duties that lay ahead.

Washington had to worry about a hundred and one details . . . keeping accounts, paying the soldiers, building barracks, making everything sanitary, salting beef for winter use—and sending endless reports to the fussy Dinwiddie. All this in addition to the main business of chasing away scalping parties!

Whenever men, money and materials failed to arrive, Washington's patience wore thin. He had always suffered from a quick temper.

His duties took him to Alexandria the time he got into a terrible argument over politics. It was Election Day, and Washington was rooting for his good friend

George William Fairfax for the House of Burgesses. A short man named William Payne favored another candidate. They had quite a fuss about it in an inn.

People gasped when Payne seized a big stick and knocked Virginia's greatest soldier to the floor. Washington got to his feet, hot with anger. He strode off ominously. Surely, thought everyone, this means a duel.

Alone in his room, Washington clenched his fists until the knuckles grew white. He was forcing himself to wait before he acted . . . to weigh the quarrel from every angle. He remembered how often in the past he had lost his temper. If he was to be severe with others, he must be more so with himself.

Next day Washington did what he thought honor called for. He met Payne and told the smaller man: "I was wrong yesterday and I apologize. Will you forget it, my plucky friend, and join me over a bowl of punch?"

The tall man held out his hand. The short man gripped it firmly. Washington made a lifelong friend. He also won a victory over himself.

There was no false humility about Washington when he honestly believed himself in the right. The old annoyance about English officers outranking colonials came up again. A certain Captain Dagworthy appeared at Fort Cumberland. He had some old captain's papers from the King. So he claimed the right to give orders to Washington and his men.

The Virginia commander-in-chief kept his temper but resolved to have a prompt showdown. It was winter now. There would be no more Indian raids till spring. He would go to Boston and put the case before Governor Shirley, who commanded all the King's troops against the French in the New World.

It was quite a winter's journey to icy New England by horseback. But matters must be settled once and for all. Washington traveled with two officers and two servants for companions. He spent his twenty-fourth birthday in Philadelphia. It was the largest city he had ever seen. Here he visited the best tailors, determined to appear his best in the coming interview.

In New York the traveler was the guest of a fellow Virginian who had married the wealthy heiress Miss Susannah Philipse. Washington quite lost his heart to her sister Mary. He took the two young ladies to a display of marvels that was the talk of the city. These included make-believe birds, ships and musicians, all moving by cogs and wheels—and acting out scenes as real as life. Such things had seldom been seen before.

George had to hurry on, but he did not forget the younger Miss Philipse. It was his luck, though, to have to keep on fighting Indians for three more weary years. By then Mary had given her hand to another.

In Boston Washington bought more hats and suits and gloves. He made a fine impression on Governor Shirley. When he went back to the frontier he took a letter saying that he—not Dagworthy—was to give the orders.

He did not return a moment too soon. As fast as the snows melted in the April sun, Indians with war hatchets swarmed over the country. Whole families of pioneers were tortured and slain—or carried off as captives.

The militia was called up for duty. But even a whisper that Indians were near was enough to make many of the militiamen break and run. The regular soldiers were little better. Mostly they were homeless wanderers or bonded servants working out their passage money to America. Having come this far, however, they did not want to lose their scalps. Even the officers were not very dependable.

"Discipline is the soul of an army," the commander-in-chief reminded them again and again. How could there be discipline, with gambling and carousing going on—and men deserting all the time?

The burgesses who told Washington it was his duty to defend Virginia were slow in voting money to pay the troops. But they were quick with blame when things went wrong.

Without an army worthy of the name, it was useless to think of counterattacking. But as 1756 and then 1757 passed, the patient Washington built a little army that at least wouldn't run away.

The war against the French was going slowly in the North, too. But finally a new minister named William Pitt came to power in England and sent over General Forbes for another attack on Fort Duquesne.

Forbes decided to build a road across Pennsylvania to the French fort. Washington helped build a road over the Alleghenies on Pennsylvania soil . . . a rival to his own Virginia route built with so much blood and sweat.

As November advanced, however, it did not seem possible that the new attack route could be ready before another winter set in. They were still many miles away when an Indian scout rushed in with amazing news.

Fort Duquesne was afire!

A party was sent out to investigate. The news was true. The proud fort at the forks of the rivers, where George had stood six years ago, was a mass of smoldering embers. The French had lost heart after setbacks elsewhere. They chose to abandon Fort Duquesne rather than stand and fight.

The fort would rise again. But this time it would have an English name and be Fort Pitt.

Washington now put his military career behind him, as he thought, forever. He had done his duty.

The frontiers of Virginia were safe. Now he could settle down and live quietly as a gentleman farmer.

For many months he had been getting ready to be a civilian. While he was still in the army, friends at Winchester put up his name for the House of Burgesses. He could not leave his post to wage a campaign. But he won anyway—and over three rivals.

As time permitted, the commander waged another kind of campaign . . . in a field where he had often met defeat. He was laying siege to a lady's heart. And this time he was playing to win.

Sometimes the army's business took him to Williamsburg. Then the commander-in-chief paused, if only for a few hours, at a delightful spot on the Pamunkey River, only thirty miles away. At homes of friends in the neighborhood, and later at the White House plantation, he paid his respects to the charming young widow Mrs. Martha Dandridge Custis.

She was not an entire stranger. The Custises moved in the gay circles Washington was apt to frequent when he stayed in the colonial capital. Before his death Mr. Custis had been a burgess, as Washington was now to be. He was a man of much influence in the affairs of Virginia—the owner of fifteen thousand acres of tobacco lands and many slaves.

Now the task of managing this big estate rested on the tiny shoulders of the little widow. When Washington gazed into the hazel eyes and frank, round face of the lovely lady, carrying herself so proudly, he knew that she had spirit and courage.

Like George, Martha was twenty-six. She was not at all like those giddy girls who had laughed at his youthful efforts to stammer out some gallantry. Four times she had been a mother. Twice she had lost a child and now she was a widow. She had lived enough to place a proper value on a man's real character.

Who in all Virginia had better proved his mettle than the tall and courteous soldier who now bowed to kiss her hand? What more could a lady with many problems—and a heart still young—look for in a husband? Who would make a more loving father for six-year-old Jacky and little Patsy?

Washington always had a present in his saddlebags for the two children. They pressed close to his chair in the elegant drawing room, begging for stories of the wild Indian country. Patsy was soon perched on his knee, with Jacky on the hassock at his feet. They looked for all the world like little grownups, the boy in his satin waistcoat and silver-buckled shoes, his little sister in tight bodice and flowing skirts. They grew wide eyed with wonder to hear of a world so strange and far away.

Martha's fingers flew over the keys of the harpsichord. There was peace in her heart as she glanced at the pleasant scene from the corner of her eye.

Soon the commander was sending to London for

china, glassware and a service of silver with the Washington family crest. The repairs he ordered were working wonders in Mount Vernon, changing it from a bachelor establishment into a home of charm.

Then one fine day Washington took his quill in hand and wrote to his English merchants—asking them to send him "enough blue velvet to make a coat, waistcoat and breeches for a tall man, with a fine silk button to suit it." They were also to send him "six pairs of the very neatest shoes and six pairs of gloves."

On January 6, 1759, George and Martha became man and wife.

Washington was a soldier no longer. He was one of the lawmakers of the colony. The hardships of the frontier were behind him now. The newlyweds reached Williamsburg for a brilliant social season.

At the races and the theater the young couple moved among friends who wished them well. The Washingtons often entertained at Martha's town home, called the Six Chimney House. In this gay company George sometimes danced the night away.

He took his bride to Mount Vernon in April, first laying in a supply of chickens and eggs and telling the servants to rub the furniture well. It was cherry blossom time when Martha caught the first glimpse of her new home. A new life was beginning for them both.

Chapter 9: MOUNT VERNON'S NO. 1 FARMER

GEORGE WASHINGTON was not much of a smoking man. When in the days gone by his Indian friends passed around the pipe of peace, he took a puff or two for politeness' sake, trying not to make a wry face. Europeans, though, looked with favor on the New World weed that was called tobacco. They smoked it. They chewed it. Fine gentlemen carried the powdered leaf in jewel-set boxes and called it snuff.

The best tobacco came from Virginia. The big tobacco market was in London. So Washington turned his attention to raising tobacco.

After the harvest he shipped hundreds of hogsheads

77

of the cured brown leaf from his Potomac wharf. The cargo went to his London merchants. With the tobacco went a long shopping list. As the tobacco was sold, these things were to be bought in England and shipped to the Washingtons.

Ships were few and the list was long . . . a silken gown for Martha . . . a gold-headed cane for George . . . plenty of clothing for the children, a size too large. They would grow into it by the time it came. There were presents, too. On the very first list after his marriage the loving stepfather wrote "six books for children beginning to read"—and "one fashionable dressed baby." By "baby" he meant a nice doll for Patsy.

To please his wife, Washington ordered a gilded carriage of seasoned wood—and, to please himself, some tasty tidbits like anchovies, olives and Cheddar cheese. Dozens of grubbing and weeding hoes were needed, along with axes to fell the trees and plows to break the ground. Without these implements there would be no tobacco. And without tobacco there would be no way to buy goods in London.

Yes, tobacco was really money in Virginia. The money grew from seeds as fine as dust. In early March you cleared rich new ground and made a seedbed.

Here each little plant grew six brave leaves. At setting time in early May you put them out in rows, leaving plenty of room between the plants.

Between the rows there was space for men to work both sides. And how much work there was to do! At resetting time you put in a new plant where one had died. Then hoeing time and weeding time—and worming time, too, for yanking off fat green pests that wanted tobacco without paying for it. There was suckering time for pulling off leaves of little promise, topping time to keep the plant from going to flower and seed. By June the tobacco was knee high. By July it was hip high.

The black field hands worked from sun to sun. Tobacco was a heavy feeder. Two or three years of it mined the soil and made it poor. Two or three acres of it took all the strength that one man had. But why worry, most Virginians asked. There were always more land beyond the Blue Ridge and more slave ships from the coast of Africa.

As time went on, Washington was to wonder whether this was a right way of thinking. Right now other things were on his mind. He must move the stripped leaves to the drying house. After that he had to put the cured tobacco into the hogsheads, ready for the ship. To raise as much tobacco as possible, he divided the Mount Vernon plantation into five farms, each with an overseer.

The big overseer was Washington himself. He rose early. His breakfast was tea and piping hot corn bread dipped in honey. For hours he was in the saddle,

making the rounds of all the farms and giving orders
to the hands. He was never too proud to get down
and put his own strong hands to the task. Not until
two or three o'clock in the afternoon could he sit
down to a leisurely dinner. Then he might linger at
the table for an hour or two over a bowl of nuts, chat-
ting with some sociable neighbor.

Mostly the talk was of crops and neighborhood
events. It might be about public affairs, for Washington, besides being a burgess, was a justice of the peace
and a vestryman of near-by Pohick Church. At these
times the bigger world seemed far away. A young
king came to the throne in England to reign as
George III. After the war with France was won, his
empire took in the lands of the Ohio and Canada as
well . . . even India on the other side of the world.

When Washington's thoughts turned to London
now, it was mostly to wonder when some sailing
vessel would drop anchor at the wharf, bringing his
long-awaited goods. He was impatient to get that
book on the latest farming methods. It was called
Horse-Hoeing Husbandry and was said to tell of
better ways to plow and cultivate. If there were better
ways, Washington wanted to know of them.

The book about horses and hoes was indeed most
helpful. The "fashionable dressed baby" caused Patsy
to fling her arms about her stepfather's neck and kiss

his cheek. But along with joyful surprises, the crates from London also brought disappointments.

Many of the farm tools were missing. They would have to be ordered over again. There would be more long months of waiting. A fishing net came without leads, corks or ropes. It was useless that way. Dishes were broken, some of the clothes fitted badly—and how in the world could a man with Washington's huge feet get into those tiny shoes with pointed toes?

Washington wrote a sharp letter to the London merchants. "Instead of getting good and fashionable things, we often have articles sent us that could only have been used by our forefathers in the days of yore," he said.

The great carriage looked very fine at first, but turned out to be the biggest disappointment of all. The family drove to church in it behind four handsome bays. Two mounted outriders in scarlet livery each guided a span of blooded horses. The carriage did not remain a thing of splendor long. The gilding fell off and the panels split.

Washington was really furious when he received a statement of his account. He had taken special care to scent his tobacco and pack it neatly. Yet it was sold at a low price as a poorer grade. The high prices charged him for his goods left him actually in debt after a year's hard work.

He turned to Martha for sympathy. "We sell cheap

and buy dear," he said. "It will not always be so. Someday we shall manufacture goods for our own needs in this country. Then we'll rely no longer on trashy merchandise from overseas."

He was fast losing his enthusiasm for tobacco. Gullies were forming in some of the best fields at Mount Vernon. The crop became smaller—and no wonder! First the land was stripped of trees, then hard-feeding tobacco plants sucked out the nourishment. Now rains were washing away the topsoil.

This would never do. Washington could not bear to see his property run down. To rest and restore the hurt land he sowed clover, alfalfa and other grasses. He prepared a compost box and marked it off into ten sections. In each of them he made up a different soil mixture, then in each he planted three grains of wheat, three of oats and three of barley. The blades grew best where there was fertilizer and black mold.

Washington learned much from experiments like these. As the seasons went by he planted less tobacco and more wheat. On one of the creeks of the estate he built a gristmill and made flour. The mill also served the people of the neighborhood. When a farmer brought in his wheat, the mill would keep one eighth of the flour for pay. Finally Washington had so much flour that he was shipping the very best grade to the West Indies for sale. It was much better than sending tobacco to London.

At Guston Hall, one of the mansions on the Potomac shore, lived George Mason. Washington came to appreciate the lively mind of this good neighbor.

"We Virginians would do well, Colonel Washington, to be sufficient unto ourselves," said Mason as they talked one day. "As long as we raise only tobacco, and depend on the London merchants for goods, they have us at their mercy."

Soon Washington was following Mason's example. Mount Vernon became a cluster of little industries, with a blacksmith's shop for forging tools, a kiln for firing bricks—and coopers busy making barrel staves. Beams and planks were hewn out and used to build boats for hire and sale.

Martha Washington ran the bakeshop, the dairy house and the kitchen garden. Her biggest job was the spinnery. Here she directed the women slaves as they made flax, wool and cotton into cloth and working clothes.

Finer clothes were still ordered from London—at great expense. It was hard to raise enough good wool in Virginia. The flocks were poor. All too often wolves and hungry dogs devoured the sheep.

So Washington went to work building stronger fences and improving the breed of sheep. He believed that when Virginians spun and wove better wool they would have less need to worry about tobacco money.

Washington was becoming an all-around livestock

breeder. He raised cattle and pigs, race horses and hunting dogs. When an animal was in trouble, he could set a broken leg or cure the mange. He counted his pets by the hundreds, giving each one a name. The horses answered to names like Magnolia, Sampson and Traveler. When Lady had four puppies he called them Vulcan, Searcher, Rover, and Sweetlips.

The shore of the Potomac was one big fishery. When there was a run of shad or herring, the catch was salted down in barrels to help feed the family and the slaves through the winter. Each year Mount Vernon's orchards bore better fruit. Washington grew skillful in grafting new varieties of pears, plums and apples on old parent stocks.

Comparing ideas one evening, Washington and Mason were happy that they no longer needed to raise tobacco, except a little to use at home. The time this jealous crop demands they now used to make things that would cost dearly in London.

"But I fear, neighbor Washington, that the King's ministers have other plans afoot to make us pay for the recent French war." Mason's tone was grave.

The two men were talking of recent events in Massachusetts. Trouble was brewing in Boston, bad trouble.

Chapter 10: A TIME FOR SPEECHES

IF TOBACCO prices made Virginia fretful, sugar and molasses had Boston in an uproar. New England's stony soil grew hardly enough grain to feed her people. But every hillside was covered with lordly trees. Skilled hands made the trees into masts and keels for fishing boats. Soon there was cod enough for all of Boston—and some to spare. So trading ships, called merchantmen, were built to carry fish and timber to West Indian markets. Sugar and molasses were taken in exchange. No vessels were fleeter, no sailing masters more daring, no merchants more ambitious than those of Boston.

Suddenly all this prosperity was threatened. Even in Virginia George Mason and George Washington were talking about "writs of assistance."

With these legal papers, British revenue cutters chased the merchantmen on the seas, stopping them and seizing their cargoes. The King's officers pushed their way into stores and warehouses, even into people's homes, looking for molasses and sugar. They wanted to know whether the taxes on them had been paid.

"Our Boston friends are said to be clever smugglers," Washington observed. "You can hardly blame them, England has winked at the sugar and molasses trade for so many years. To enforce the law at this late date means the ruin of Boston's trade."

"More than that." Mason's eyes kindled. "It means the end of a precious English freedom. When a man's home can be entered this way, the innocent suffer with the guilty. Mark my words, Colonel, we shall hear more of this before it is over."

More of it Washington did hear—at the very next meeting of the House of Burgesses. This time tax money was demanded of all the colonies. A Stamp Act was coming. Every legal paper, every newspaper, would soon be taxed. The mother country said her children must help pay for whipping the French.

The plan brought angry words from the younger burgesses. Hadn't the colonies done their full share

to lick them. Newspapers stopped publication or came out boldly with a skull and crossbones where the stamp was meant to be. Angry crowds told the tax collectors to resign—or else seized the stamps and burned them.

Happily, a turn for the better came the following year. New ministers entered the King's service. The Stamp Act was repealed. Now Washington could leave the scenes of angry debate for his peaceful fields of grain and clover. How much pleasanter to be with Martha and the children . . . to pass gay evenings with warmhearted neighbors . . . to rise with the dawn and ride after a fox with horses and dogs.

It was all too good to last. Once more there were changes in London and new tax laws for the colonies. This time the tax was on glass, paper, paints and tea.

Soon the master of Mount Vernon was to read the *Virginia Gazette* with a furrowed brow. The proud sloop *Liberty* had been seized for smuggling. "There'll be trouble in Boston," he said.

This vessel belonged to the great merchant John Hancock. And it was not long before Hancock's friends dragged the British revenue officers ashore and set their cutter on fire. One thing led to another. Two regiments of redcoats were sent to scare the unruly Bostonians. Next time, they were told, they would be taken to England for trial, far from their homes and friends.

These happenings seemed so serious that Washington wrote to his neighbor Mason. "Our lordly masters in Great Britain will be satisfied with nothing less than depriving us of liberty," he declared. "It seems highly necessary that something should be done. No man should hesitate to use arms in defense of so valuable a blessing. Yet arms should be the last resort."

The two men met and talked gravely. Together they wrote a paper. Washington carried it with him to the House of Burgesses that spring of 1769.

It took no fiery talks this time to pass a resolution. The burgesses made a sharp protest against the new taxes and the new threats. To the royal governor Lord Botetourt this was an insult to the King. He told the Virginia lawmakers to leave the capital and go home. They were fired.

The burgesses were in no mood to be silenced and scattered. So they hired the Apollo Room at the Raleigh Tavern. This gaily painted banquet hall was a favorite spot of Williamsburg society. Many a toast had been drunk here to the King. But a different kind of business brought these grim-faced Virginians here today. At the proper time Washington pulled out the paper on which he and Mason had worked.

"Gentlemen, I wish to propose a nonimportation agreement," he said, going on to explain what this was. "If we refuse to buy English goods, and get our neighbors to do the same, perhaps the King's ministers will come to their senses. Surely it is better to do without London finery than give up our ancient liberties."

Then and there the representatives of Virginia's greatest families made a solemn pledge. They set their names to a list of things they wouldn't buy until the trouble with England was over. Slaves were one item on Washington's list. Their sale brought rich profit to English traders. But slavery was a doubtful blessing to the Virginia planters.

This was an illegal gathering of rebellious subjects, in the royal governor's eyes. Yet from that day on, the meeting in the Apollo Room has been treasured as one of Virginia's most glorious moments.

No more pretty clothes from London reached Mount Vernon, but the loyal Martha made no complaint. The Washington family could dress in homespun all right, but let it be the best. Soon this capable lady had a score of spindles and looms at work. Her spinnery turned out linen and woolen cloth, besides a mixture of the two—called linsey-woolsey.

There was room on this continent for a nation to grow so great no chains could hold it down. The Washingtons realized this when they traveled to the warm springs in western Virginia with Miss Patsy. She was a lovable child of twelve now, but her frail body was shaken at times by disease. It was almost more than her parents could bear—to see her suffer . . . to try every means of healing . . . then to find that nothing seemed to help.

The following year business took Washington still farther west. He went to the Ohio Valley to stake out land claims. He and his fellow officers had earned these by fighting in the French and Indian War. Traveling with his friend Dr. Craik and two servants, Washington visited Fort Necessity, the place of his first defeat, and Logstown, where he had talked with the redskins. Then the party took to canoes and paddled far, far down the Ohio to the mouth of the Great Kanawha River. For food they shot deer and wild turkeys. An Indian gave them a quarter of delicious buffalo meat.

Often they saw herds of these shaggy animals. Washington tried to figure out a way of getting some of the calves to Mount Vernon so he could raise tame buffaloes. They would make a new and useful domestic animal—one that was quite American.

Washington picked out choice bottom land along these rivers for many miles. The land seemed so far away that—when he returned—some of the soldiers were glad to sell him their pieces. Before long he had thirty-two thousand acres of these western lands.

But though he prospered with his property, Washington had reason to worry for his children and his country. Every postrider brought more news of trouble in Boston. At home Patsy's illness grew no better. And Jacky was shooting up to tall manhood with all too little schooling and serious purpose.

He had an open heart and a generous nature, along with a lively interest in dogs, horses, guns and clothes. However, he found Latin and mathematics quite dreary. His tutors gave up in despair. Then his stepfather placed Jacky in a school at Annapolis, Maryland, hoping he would be made to study.

All that happened was that young Master Custis fell in love with the sister of a schoolmate. Miss Nelly Calvert was a charming girl, but she and Jacky were too young to marry, Washington insisted. Jacky should master his studies first. He would have a large estate to manage someday—and yet, at nineteen, he could not even figure well!

So the marriage was postponed. Washington set out with his stepson to King's College in New York, soon to be renamed Columbia by a people who no longer loved their King. Jacky, still daydreaming about his Nelly, was enrolled here as a student.

It was June when Washington returned to Mount Vernon. One summer evening shortly after that, Patsy rose gaily from the table. Martha and George remarked that she looked better than usual. A moment later, to their horror, she was seized by an attack of her illness and passed away almost as soon as they could reach her side.

In the weeks that followed, Washington tried to comfort the sorrowing Martha.

"The sweet, innocent girl is relieved of her suffering," he told her. But it seemed as though the mother's heart would never mend. Nelly Calvert was a frequent guest at Mount Vernon that summer and fall. Her welcome visits helped Martha endure the loss of Patsy.

Not only were Jacky and Nelly lonely for each other, but Martha begged for a chance to see her boy. Tugging at a button of her husband's coat, she looked up into his face imploringly. This was more than Washington could resist. The stern lines softened— his stepson was allowed to come home from school.

The young couple were married that winter at the bride's home in Annapolis. Jacky's mother was too deep in mourning to attend. So she placed a message to "My Dear Nelly" in Washington's hands.

"God took from me a daughter when June roses were blooming," it read. "He has now, when winter winds are blowing, given me another daughter, about her age, to warm my heart again."

Chapter 11: A TIME FOR ACTION

To WASHINGTON'S FAMILY cares were added the nation's woes. American blood was shed on Boston streets. The beach at Dorchester was strewn with British tea.

A broadside telling of the Boston Massacre came into Washington's hands. A picture by Paul Revere showed a line of redcoats firing on peaceful citizens. Some of them lay dead or wounded on the ground.

In Boston, feelings had run high. No one liked having British soldiers about. Cries of "Lobster Back" and worse greeted the unwelcome guests on their rounds. Washington was not there to see the hotheaded crowd taunt the King's men until they quite lost their patience. His Virginia blood boiled at this picture of men falling in the cause of American liberty.

The master of Mount Vernon did not know their names . . . not even the name of Crispus Attucks, the first of all to die. But he looked upon the bleeding man and suffered with him. The face in the drawing was a sort of white lie. The Massachusetts men feared to tell the slaveholding South that Attucks, the first of the patriot dead, was a free Negro with a black skin.

By the time of the Boston Tea Party there was a Committee of Correspondence in Virginia to speed the news. Through committees like this, secret letters passed quickly from colony to colony over a kind of grapevine.

How the British feared the magic vine as it drew thirteen separate colonies into a single network! "Serpents from the eggs of sedition," they called the secret letters—meaning by this that the minds of the people were being poisoned against their rightful King. The serpent, they said, had his head in Massachusetts. And the tongue of the serpent was the acid pen of Samuel Adams. For it was he who started the Committees of Correspondence.

That is why the British insisted on landing tea at Boston Harbor. They would give up the tax on everything else. But the tax on tea must remain. Boston would be made to pay it. And Sam Adams, if he did not take care, would hang.

Washington heard how men disguised as Indians dumped the fragrant chests of tea into the bay. He didn't like the idea of destroying property. Yet he knew that Boston's cause was also Virginia's. This time Britain would strike back hard, he said.

How true this proved to be! When England's blow fell there was no time to wait for letters. A courier from the North came dashing into Williamsburg asking the burgesses to stand with Massachusetts in her coming hour of trial. British warships were to close the port of Boston on June 1st. It would stay closed until the tea was paid for. Freedom-loving Massachusetts was to lose her charter of rights. Town meetings, where everyone could have his say, were to be curbed. More redcoats were on the way. And they could be quartered in people's homes, like it or not.

All this was bad enough, especially for Massachusetts. But then came something that hit right home to Washington and his neighbors. All the western lands upon the Ohio were taken away and made a part of Canada. What would happen to the hard-earned land claims of hundreds of Virginians? No one knew.

These were called the Intolerable Acts. They were more than the colonists could bear.

Thomas Jefferson, now sitting in the House of Burgesses, offered a resolution making June 1st a day of fasting and prayer. This, he hoped, would "give the American people one heart and one mind to oppose every injury to American rights."

So on June 1, 1774, flags were at half-mast in Virginia as the blockade of Boston Harbor began. Church bells tolled across the countryside.

More and more the colonists called themselves Americans now.

"An empire," Samuel Adams wrote, "is rising in America. Boston suffers with dignity. The virtue of our ancestors inspires us. They were contented with clams and mussels."

But though not a ship could move, Boston did not have to go hungry. To send in food, Washington signed his name at the top of a list and made a gift of fifty pounds. A South Carolina planter sent a load of rice with the message, "Don't pay for an ounce of the tea!" Israel Putnam drove in a flock of sheep from Connecticut. The fishermen of Marblehead, across the bay, brought their catch by wagon to Boston.

In July Washington sat in the chair when the voters of Fairfax County met. Americans must learn to make the things they used, he argued. Let neighbor help neighbor to build up better flocks of sheep so there would be more wool to spin and weave.

These same ideas were taken up when the burgesses met in August. The colonies knew at last that they must all become good neighbors. There was to be a

Continental Congress in Philadelphia the following month. All thirteen provinces would act together as one people in this hour of crisis. Virginia voted to send seven delegates, among them Washington.

The former colonel had a few words to say to the burgesses. Usually he was slow to speech, but now he rose to his full height and spoke in a firm voice.

"I will raise one thousand men, care for them at my own expense and march at their head for the relief of Boston," George Washington offered.

It was not a long speech but it was listened to like one of Patrick Henry's. It promised action. And the time for action was coming.

"I hope you stand firm. I know George will."

On the veranda at Mount Vernon Martha Washington was saying good-by to Patrick Henry and Edmund Pendleton as they left with her husband for Philadelphia.

This was the home of the wise Ben Franklin. "Join or die," he had once told the colonies, claiming they could no more remain apart than a snake could live in thirteen pieces. At last they were heeding his advice. As Washington and his companions started out, fully fifty delegates headed toward Philadelphia.

Franklin would not be there. He was in England trying, though now with little hope, to make peace with the mother country. The Fairfaxes were now in

Britain, too. Washington knew from them that the American cause had many friends, but unfortunately these friends were not in power.

The delegates met at Carpenters' Hall. Never before had so many important Americans met together and sized one another up.

"I am not a Virginian, I am an American," cried Patrick Henry in pride.

Many now felt, and Washington among them, that it was too late for petitions to the King. But others insisted on one more warning. The wise Boston lawyer John Adams compared America to a fleet sailing under convoy. The fastest sailers must wait for the dullest and slowest.

Some people said the Adamses were wild and rash. Washington was surprised to hear how reasonably they talked. They were cousins—and even Cousin Sam made a respectable appearance. True, the man whose pen was like a serpent's sting had hardly a shilling to his name. But his friends had just bought him a new suit of clothes so he would make a good impression on the rich Virginians.

Peyton Randolph of Virginia was chairman of this First Continental Congress. Not everyone noticed another Virginian who listened quietly and said little. Washington was more apt to speak his mind around the dinner table or on a stroll about State House Square. As he made friends, however, his words were appreciated. No man, as Patrick Henry noted, was more respected for his solid judgment. As yet, Washington had no idea of independence. He just wanted the colonies to have their rights.

When Washington came home from Philadelphia, armed companies were forming in various counties. The riflemen of a western company could pierce an apple at two hundred yards. First one company, then others sent committees to Mount Vernon to ask its owner to be their commander.

George Washington had not commanded troops for fifteen years. He had hoped to remain a peaceful farmer all his days. And now here he was again at forty-two . . . back in uniform, calling out orders, buying all the muskets, powder horns and bullet bags he could find. He wore a uniform of buff and blue, the colors of his Fairfax County command. He was to wear it for nine long years.

History moved now with a giant's stride. A convention was held at Richmond early in 1775. These men came stripped for action. Instead of wigs and ruffles they wore hunting shirts. Muskets rested against their knees. It was here that Patrick Henry cried, "If we wish to be free, we must fight. I know not what course others may take, but as for me, give me liberty—or give me death!"

Washington was placed on committees to arm soldiers in every county and to encourage the making of wool, cotton, linen and gunpowder. Without American manufactures there could be no American rights.

Soon there were skirmishes over the colony's store of powder. The royal governor was forced to flee to a British man-of-war.

The Continental Congress was to meet again in Philadelphia in May. Just as Washington was leaving, word reached Mount Vernon that war had actually broken out at Lexington and Concord. The British General Gage had sent out a troop of scarlet grenadiers from Boston to seize the rebels' store of ammunition. But the colonists, roused by Paul Revere, stood their ground when fired upon. The redcoats went scurrying back to Boston under cover of walls and fences, ducking fire from the shotguns of angry farmers.

The uniform of buff and blue made Washington's tall figure stand out still more at the Continental Congress. It was a good garb to wear, for this Second Continental Congress met in time of war.

Word arrived that Ethan Allen of Vermont and his Green Mountain boys had made the British surrender Fort Ticonderoga "in the name of the Great Jehovah and the Continental Congress."

Actually the Congress had no army. But outside of Boston an army of minutemen and volunteers was springing up. To what colony did this army belong? To Massachusetts? No, for fighting men were swarming in from Connecticut, Rhode Island and New Hampshire as well. It was an American army.

Who would command it? A New Englander? New England men were doing the fighting so far, but help from the southern colonies—and especially Virginia—was needed, too. All this while John Adams was asking the southern delegates whom they preferred for commander-in-chief. He was putting the same question to the northern delegates, but also he was telling them that it would be smart to have a southern general—to help bind the colonies together.

Everyone spoke of the tall man with the firm-set jaw and the uniform of buff and blue.

On June 14, 1775, John Adams made a famous speech. It was high time, he declared, for Congress to adopt the army outside of Boston and name a general.

"I have but one gentleman in mind for that important command," Adams continued. "He is a gentleman from Virginia who is among us and very well known to us all. He has skill as an officer, an independent fortune, great talents and excellent character. Better than any other person in the Union, he can unite all the colonies."

At this, Washington, from a sense of modesty, hurried from the room. Next day he was unanimously elected commander-in-chief of the new army. He rose to offer his humble thanks.

"I do not think myself equal to the command I am

honored with," said George Washington, modestly.

The new commander refused a salary. For mere money he would never leave his happy home.

"I will keep an exact account of my expenses," he explained. "This is all I desire."

The hardest thing was to break the news to Martha. There was no time to return to Mount Vernon.

"You may believe me that I tried to avoid this appointment," he wrote. "It has been a kind of destiny—and I hope it is meant to answer some good purpose."

There was a great send-off for the commander-in-chief as he rode north, erect in his saddle, into his unknown destiny. Bands played . . . there was a mounted escort . . . and delegates in fine carriages saw him on his way.

The second day a horseman came dashing up to Washington in a cloud of dust. All out of breath, he was trying to tell of a great battle between the red-coats and the colonists. It was hard to make head or tail of it, he was so excited. But it happened on Bunker Hill.

"Tell me one thing," Washington broke in. "Did the militia fight?"

"Yes, Your Excellency, they stood their ground. As long as they had powder left."

A sigh of relief came from the commander. "Then the liberties of the country are safe," he said.

Chapter 12: A VIRGINIAN AMONG THE YANKEES

UNDER A LOFTY ELM a tall figure in blue and buff sat on a white charger. Straight and grave as an Indian, he lifted his sword, returning the salute of the Continental Army.

It was July 3, 1775, a bright and sunny day. A huge throng was watching the general take over his new command. Across Cambridge Common was Harvard College. Below, the land sloped to the Charles River. Downstream lay Boston, where the British were. A white-columned mansion with a neat garden was given to General Washington for his headquarters. The owner, a British sympathizer, a Tory, had fled from the angry patriots.

Beyond a few streets of humbler houses lay farms and fields of grain. Washington's army was encamped out there . . . the men who had sprung to arms after Lexington and Concord, Massachusetts men and brave fellows like Nathanael Greene, the blacksmith from Rhode Island, and Israel Putnam, who hurried to battle from his Connecticut farm without even taking off his leather apron.

The British, since the terrible losses they took at Bunker Hill, were only too glad to hole up in Boston. But Washington knew that not all his soldiers were heroes. There were those who had run away. Even some officers were on trial for cowardice. Tough discipline was needed, he could see, to turn these farm boys and mechanics into real soldiers.

The camp's disgraceful appearance made the general scowl. A wonder the fever wasn't raging—with all this litter about! And look at those old boards from rubbish heaps nailed together to form ramshackle huts. The only tents were those the mariners made from their own sailcloth. Washington made a note to ask Congress for a supply.

His list was growing long. Uniforms were needed, or warm clothing at the very least. These men had come from the plow or the workbench. A few had captured odds and ends of British uniforms. Some, from the western hills, did not even have shirts but wore blankets instead.

Yet it was a great outpouring of people. Young and old stood together. It was startling to an owner of slaves to see black faces in the ranks among the white. Washington later grew used to this and learned to value the Negro troops who served him through a long war.

In New England, too, a shoemaker or an innkeeper could command a company. He might even be elected by their vote. Washington's brow darkened when he came upon a captain running a razor over the lathered chin of a common soldier.

"I was a barber before. Why shouldn't I be a barber now?" asked the puzzled officer.

To Washington this meant poor discipline. And discipline, he always said, is the soul of an army.

Yet how could you discipline these stubborn Yankees? If you pushed them too hard they would leave at night and be over the hills by morning. Wasn't this a free man's right? If not, what was all the fighting about? That was the way the New Englanders talked.

"My life is one continuous round of annoyance," the weary Washington wrote a friend. His worries multiplied as the year went by. The colonies were slow to send more soldiers and quick to give high rank to ambitious officers. Colonels and generals kept showing up in camp, arguing over the claims of other colonies and sulking if they couldn't have their way.

"Every post ought to be deemed honorable in which a man can serve his country." This was Washington's rebuke to a fretting officer.

All this time Washington bore the burden of a dreadful secret . . . a secret he couldn't even share with his fellow officers or write to Congress in a letter. It might fall into the hands of the enemy. The army was down to thirty-two barrels of powder—only enough for a round or two of firing if the redcoats attacked in force. The commander's face was like a thundercloud when a careless soldier fired his musket in the air just for fun. Why, America's very freedom might depend on that precious powder!

General Washington was expected to entertain the important people of New England at his headquarters. Often he rose from the table and excused himself, leaving an aide to do honors to the guests. Retiring to a candlelit study he spent hours on careful reports to Congress. "Hurry those tents and stocks of clothing before winter sets in," he begged. "Send more arms—and quickly. Above all, send powder."

He knew Congress was few in number and overworked. Yet how slow they were with help!

All this while, know-it-alls sat in chimney corners and complained. Why didn't Washington attack the

British in Boston? The general must be a do-nothing. Maybe he was afraid of the redcoats. Washington had to grit his teeth and bear it. How could he tell the armchair generals how little powder he had?

Washington did have high hopes on one score, though. Brave General Montgomery was off for Montreal in Canada. And now Benedict Arnold had started up the Kennebec to join him near Quebec. It was a daring deed—to lead a force of men through the Maine woods in the dead of winter. Yet what a blow for freedom it would be to win Canada to the cause of the United Colonies. After that there need be no fear of Britain taking over the Hudson River and the lakes north of it.

Washington had figured out the British plan . . . to hold a line from New York to Canada and so cut off New England from the other colonies. New England was the head of the serpent, in English eyes. This would lop off the serpent's head.

The wise old serpent would be no easy target. But to come out with a whole skin he would have to be crafty—and patient, too.

A long struggle lay ahead before the master of Mount Vernon could sit by his own fireside. Martha longed to be with him—and he with her. There were whispers of a British plot to send a cruiser up the Potomac and seize Mrs. Washington as a hostage. Hearing this, the commander no longer hesitated but sent for his wife to join him at the Cambridge camp.

Martha set out by carriage in December. It was a cold journey but she felt the warmth of friendship at every town. Escorts turned out to honor the commander's wife. By the time Mrs. Washington reached Cambridge she was Lady Washington. And she was in time to see a new flag raised over her husband's headquarters. It was the banner of the United Colonies. A Union Jack was in the upper corner, while flanking it were thirteen stripes, seven of red and six of white.

Washington and his wife were together on their seventeenth wedding anniversary. It was a new experience for the little lady to live on the edge of a battlefield and hear the cannon roar. Yet how happy she was to be with her general and lighten his burdens even a little. And with her gracious hospitality she quite won the hearts of the New Englanders.

As 1776 began, Washington's army was smaller than the one of the year before—and there were new faces. Some old faces were there, too . . . faces of men brave enough to stick it out for another year.

To Washington it seemed that no sooner did he drill a little order into his men than they were gone and he must start with others. He pleaded for an army that would serve until the war was over. But long enlistments were not popular.

In another way, though, 1776 was a turning point. It was the year when Americans realized, with sorrow, that they must part from Britain. Parliament had refused even to hear the petition of Congress. The King made an angry speech vowing to bend the Americans to his will. He signed his royal name to a law closing every port in the colonies. He ordered American ships seized and their crews put to work. Some of them were forced to fight against their own countrymen. Falmouth, Maine, was burned by British raiders. Then Norfolk, Virginia, was put to the torch, while women and children fled in the cold night under a naval bombardment.

So Washington, who had hoped for peace and making up, turned at last against his King. He liked the ideas in a new pamphlet called *Common Sense*, by Thomas Paine.

"It is absurd for a continent to be governed by an island," Thomas Paine wrote. Washington agreed. "That makes common sense," he said.

Congress now opened the ports of America to the ships of all nations except England. Yankee crews, used to hunting whales on the seven seas, now hunted English shipping. They took the enemy boats as prizes and came back with provisions and powder for Washington to use.

Good news was mixed with the bad at Cambridge. Montgomery took Montreal. Arnold, after cruel hardships, reached the St. Lawrence. The attack on Quebec was made during a snowstorm on New Year's Eve. But it turned into a tragic failure, with Montgomery killed and Arnold wounded.

In another battle with the snows the Americans did better. Oxen came lumbering in with sleds bearing the British cannon from Fort Ticonderoga. The huge guns had been dragged through snows and forests all the way from the New York wilderness between Lakes George and Champlain.

There would be important work for these guns to do! Too long Washington had been on the receiving end. Now, if he were quick enough and quiet enough, he could be on the sending end.

"If I place my troops behind stout earthworks, they will give the enemy a hot time," he told himself.

So on the night of March 4th he sent out orders that every man who could be spared should hurry to Dorchester Heights and dig as if his life depended on it. The works must be completed that very night . . . before the British learned of them.

Thousands of men toiled with pickax and spade in the darkness. Others filled barrels with stones to roll down on the redcoats if they should attack. March 5th dawned, six years to a day since the shooting on Boston streets. General Howe, the new British commander, must have rubbed his eyes as if Aladdin had been there with his magic lamp. The hills were lined with fortifications. And Ticonderoga's frowning guns were aimed right at the unbelieving British.

These heights commanded Boston from the south. Washington's guns could fire right down on the enemy. If Howe had any doubts about it, he knew now he could not hope to stay in Boston. So the redcoats made haste to go. Washington let them leave without firing on them. He didn't want to do any needless harm to the city's people. Through field glasses he saw the harbor grow thick with masts as a fleet gathered to carry the enemy away. Twenty regiments were lines of scarlet moving to the wharves. The less orderly throng behind were Loyalists who asked to go with Howe. These friends of the King were bold no longer. They were fearful of their neighbors now. Clutching a few belongings, nine hundred of these nervous Tories took ship. Most of them would never see their native land again.

Within a fortnight Boston was free. For the moment there was not a redcoat on American soil.

Congress voted a medal honoring Washington as the leader of a liberating army. Harvard College, across Cambridge Common, named him a Doctor of Laws. He was forty-four—and it was his first college degree. He had missed out on an English schooling but he had learned enough to teach the English something.

Chapter 13: FREE AND INDEPENDENT STATES

WHERE WAS HOWE? This question worried Washington all that spring of 1776. The redcoat general's fleet had sailed away from Boston. The chances were it would show up in New York, for then the redcoats could push up the Hudson to join the other English force already moving down from Canada.

How could Washington, with hardly any navy, defend New York against England's mighty sea power? Well, perhaps he couldn't, but he would make a try—and delay the foe at any rate.

It was a welcome sight to see troops coming in from Philadelphia, from New Jersey and Maryland, even from the South. The King was losing his friends with every ship that brought news from Europe. Now it was learned that he was hiring an army of Hessians. The war on the Americans was so unpopular in England that George III had to fill the ranks with these paid soldiers of a German prince.

"This is the answer to your petitions!" cried Sam Adams to those still loyal to the King.

Washington's own Virginia now came out for independence. Richard Henry Lee rose in Congress to move "that these United Colonies are, and of right ought to be, free and independent states." John Adams seconded the motion. Soon he—along with Thomas Jefferson and others—were on a committee to write a Declaration of Independence.

Washington sent Martha to Philadelphia, for with Howe's attack expected any moment, he felt she was safer there. Before June was over he was doubly glad to be facing danger without her. For there was a Loyalist plot to assassinate the commander-in-chief by serving him a dish of poisoned peas. The Tories were hated more than ever after this, and Washington did not feel so sorry for them as he had at Boston. For he loved life—and he was very fond of peas.

Late in June a British attack by sea on Charleston failed. After this, South Carolina came out for independence. The famous Declaration of July 4th followed a few days later at Philadelphia.

Though bonfires blazed and bells rang out, it was several days before the news reached New York. On the evening of July 10th Washington ordered his entire army out on parade. The declaration, saying that the American people had the right to life, liberty, and the pursuit of happiness, was read at the head of every brigade.

Now they were the United States Army. Their lives, their arms and their sacred honor were pledged to defend a new nation.

A statue of George III astride his horse seemed strangely out of place on the Bowling Green in these new circumstances. Ropes were made fast to it. Willing hands tugged until it lay broken on the grass.

"We will melt the King's statue for lead to shoot back at him," the soldiers shouted.

Washington was not amused. Next day he told the demonstrators that it was not very brave to attack a statue.

The thirteen colonies were free and independent states . . . on paper. Now it was up to Washington to make that paper good. Howe's redcoats were landing on Staten Island in New York Harbor. His brother Lord Howe, the admiral, was there a week later with an even bigger fleet and more thousands of armed men.

The English cruised about at will, scarcely noticing

Washington's feeble batteries on the shore. Surely, thought the Howes, these rebels will see that resistance is useless. They had little heart for the war and hoped to end it by a show of strength. The admiral sent a message to "George Washington, Esquire," offering peace and pardon. Lord Howe would not call him "General Washington."

The commander-in-chief refused the letter. "Those who have committed no fault want no pardon," he told the admiral's messenger.

Now he would have to fight. Where would the British land? It was a score of miles and more around Manhattan, with New York at its lower tip. And Washington had to watch Long Island, across the East River. If the British took Brooklyn Heights, over there, they could fire on New York at will.

Late in August some eight thousand redcoats went ashore on Long Island and were creeping up on Brooklyn. Washington gave General Putnam what troops he could spare to hold them back. He stayed in New York himself for fear the British would attack both places at once.

"Remember, officers and soldiers, that you are free men, fighting for the blessings of liberty." This was Washington's order of the day.

Three main approaches to Brooklyn were well defended. But there was only a light guard on the Jamaica Road, well out on Long Island. By striking their biggest blow here, the British reached the rear of the American lines. Hundreds of Americans were mowed down in the slaughter that followed. Other hundreds became prisoners.

Washington now took command in person. He was in the saddle for forty-eight hours, encouraging his men and making plans to prevent a new disaster. Heavy rain pelted the sleepless commander and his gray steed. But the rain fell on the redcoats, too. While they took shelter, Washington speeded preparations to bring his army together again in New York.

He ordered every boat able to move men hurried to the Brooklyn ferry. Hundreds of flat-bottomed craft were there the night of the 29th.

Now Washington started moving nine thousand men across a mile of water to the safety of Manhattan. It had to be a secret from the British lest they attack. It had to be a secret from the men themselves lest they take fright. In little groups, the men groped their way down the slippery steps. A storm blew up. Sails were useless. The splashing oars were muffled in rags.

At midnight the wind changed, however. Sails were hoisted to speed the passage. A cannon went off by mistake. For a moment, Washington's heart stood still. Mixed-up orders left the American lines wholly undefended for a while. Somehow, at last, every man was put safely on board.

Day had come when the last barge shoved off. Fog

hid its movement. It carried away Washington and his gray horse. When British patrols came out at last, they fired at the barge in vain. General Washington had lost a battle but he had saved an army.

With Brooklyn gone, how could New York be held? As a military man, Washington knew it would be better to burn the city to the ground. This, at least, would keep the British from having a warm place to winter in. But Congress would not hear of this, demanding that the city be defended.

"It might be possible," replied the commander-in-chief, "if the men would do their duty. But this I despair of."

A third of Washington's men were sick in body and all were sick at heart. Two months' pay was owing them. Many were leaving, taking their flintlocks and blankets with them.

Even those who stayed were frightened men as they lay in shallow trenches along the East and Hudson rivers. They stared at enemy frigates.

To escape a trap on this narrow island, Washington moved his headquarters to Harlem Heights, ten miles up the Hudson. Before he could get his men and supplies out, the British started landing.

Cannon fire at Kip's Bay drew the general to the scene of action. Speeding his battle horse through a cornfield, he beheld a sight too terrible to believe. His men were fleeing in terror. Sixty redcoats who had leaped ashore from barges were chasing them.

"Are these the men with whom I am to defend America?" the commander cried in anguish.

A towering rage came over him. He ordered the officers to form the ranks again. But they were in panic, too.

Drawing and cocking his pistol, Washington tried to force his men to stand and fight. The pistol failed to fire. He threatened them with his sword. He beat them with his riding crop. Nothing would stop them.

The British were coming—and the commander-in-chief was almost alone, so low in spirits he was ready to stay there and die. At the last moment, an aide grasped the bridle and led the general away.

After that the shame of the army was so great that British buglers mocked it with fox-hunting tunes. Tired at last of being made sport of, an American patrol turned on its tormentors. The action grew into the Battle of Harlem Heights. The British were forced back a mile or two. Just to see his men face fire gave Washington new heart.

The best he could hope for, though, with his weak force was to delay the enemy. In the hills near White Plains, farther north, General Howe attacked once more. Though a thousand of the militiamen ran at the first shot, six hundred fought till help came. For this small favor Washington was grateful. General

Charles Lee, his second in command, took part of the troops to guard the highlands of the Hudson. Washington crossed with the rest into New Jersey and came down the other bank.

Of the American defenses on the lower Hudson, only Fort Lee in New Jersey and Fort Washington across the river now remained. From the Jersey side Washington could see the enemy laying siege to the fort that was named for him.

"Hold out till night and I will take you out," was the word he sent. But the garrison, with three thousand men, surrendered that afternoon.

Four days later Washington had to give up Fort Lee, barely getting off his men.

The darkest hours he had ever known were now upon him. Winter was setting in. Washington was down to a couple of thousand men—clad in rags. All the way across the Jersey meadows, Cornwallis and his men in snug, warm coats of red were at his heels.

Washington was no longer the elegant figure who took command a year and a half ago. Even those close to him began to turn against him now. They felt he was a failure. It would be better to put the clever Lee in charge, they thought. No doubt Lee thought so, too. He paid no heed to Washington's call for help. Then one morning the British captured the careless Lee as he lingered over breakfast.

Howe offered pardons to everyone in New Jersey

who would beg for the King's mercy. Soon hundreds of Americans were flocking to the British camps to become Englishmen again. The free and independent states—so proudly proclaimed in July—seemed to be forgotten. It was now December.

Washington wrote his brother Jack, "If every nerve is not strained to recruit a new army, I think the game is pretty near up."

A few loyal patriots rummaged for old clothes to keep Washington's little army from freezing. The commander received the bundles gratefully.

A small and homely man was with the forlorn band on this flight through Jersey. He was Thomas Paine, the writer of *Common Sense*. Now he was writing another pamphlet to be called *The Crisis*. The head of a drum was Paine's desk. Here, around the lonely campfires, he wrote down his words at the end of the day's march. On these night watches, Washington would ask to hear the latest passages. By the flickering light, Paine obliged while the men listened.

"These are times that try men's souls," he read. "The summer soldier and the sunshine patriot will, in this crisis, shrink from the service of their country; but he that stands it now, deserves the love and thanks of man and woman."

Words like these were warming to the heart. Hearing them, the shivering patriot army—what little was left of it—took hope.

Chapter 14: FOOTPRINTS IN THE SNOW

IT WAS ALMOST CHRISTMAS—and anything but merry for George Washington. Most of his army would melt away on New Year's Day. Few would care to serve in 1777 when 1776 was ending so drearily.

One thing Washington knew. He would never beg for the King's pardon. If need be, he would take refuge in Virginia's western hills. From there, if only a hundred men would follow him, he would wage war on the British. He would make lightning attacks on their outposts and keep the spark of independence aglow until better days returned.

But before he was pushed to the wall, Washington

would strike one final blow. "Necessity, dire necessity, must justify any attempt," he said.

Howe had placed a garrison of Hessians in Trenton. Washington had put the waters of the Delaware between himself and them, taking all the boats over to the Pennsylvania side. As soon as the river froze, the enemy would be on his heels. Already Congress had fled from Philadelphia.

American spies brought Washington word from across the river. The men the King had hired in Germany were lonely for their native land. To cheer them up, a Christmas celebration was planned. Farms were plundered for pigs to roast. The wine would flow freely.

Following a strange German custom, saplings of evergreen were being trimmed with candles and gay colors and strung with presents. How the homesick Hessians chattered of the good cheer they would find around this greenery on Christmas Day—dining on the fat of the land and singing carols!

A Christmas tree was something new to Washington. But he had a few presents he would like to deliver in Trenton.

Not even a trench defended the town. Colonel Rall and his Hessians were just this scornful of Washington's beaten army. The commander-in-chief explained his plan, warning his generals not to breathe a word of it.

"Christmas night, an hour before dawn, is the time to strike," he told them. "The enemy will be drowsy, I warrant, after a night of carousing."

One thing more. The password. "It is Victory or Death," said the commander. "Never forget it."

On Christmas afternoon the tattered men stumbled to the ferries. Shivering in thin rags, they felt cold indeed toward the King who wouldn't let Americans manufacture woolens. Frostbitten toes stuck out of broken shoes. Some of the troops were barefoot. The path they took across the snow was marked by bloody prints.

Each man was handed forty rounds of ammunition. Horses dragged eighteen cannon to the landing. Washington sat on a chestnut sorrel while a cold wind blew—and his nose was very red. The furrows in his brow grew deeper as he saw cakes of floating ice clogging the Delaware.

Lucky these skillful fishermen from Marblehead are here to man the boats, he thought. To keep the timetable he had planned, they ought to get across by midnight. But the big watch Washington looked at anxiously by lantern light told him they would never make it. The wind became a gale. The rain beat down in torrents. Ice floes in the angry current buffeted the boats. The freezing men clutched the sides, the horses reared and plunged. It was a wonder they got the big guns across at all.

It was 3:00 A.M. when Washington reached the Jersey side. It took an hour to prepare to march. The commander sent General Sullivan by the river road. Washington and Greene took the upper road. They would meet in Trenton, nine miles south.

What a night it turned out to be! The driving rain changed to sleet. Hailstones lashed the sleepy men.

Sullivan sent word from the river road that water was ruining the ammunition and fouling the guns.

"Use the bayonet then," Washington replied. "I am resolved to take Trenton."

Feeble rays of day pierced the snowflakes. This meant there was no longer any chance of surprising the Hessians under cover of darkness. But there was no turning back now.

At eight o'clock they reached the town. Bugle calls were heard as enemy sentries gave the alarm. Bullets whizzed over Washington's head. But he smiled to hear cannon fire—a sign that Sullivan was entering Trenton, too. The dazed Hessians were tumbling from their quarters. The Americans charged quickly in the confusion.

Light horse (cavalry) were at the mouth of enemy cannon to put them out of use. The big guns Washington had babied through the ice were set up where their fire could sweep the streets.

Colonel Rall, his brain fogged with too much Christmas wine, tried to rally his Hessians. It was too late now. Americans under cover of trees and doors were picking off his men and attacking with the bayonet when they tried to form their line. A battery under the young Alexander Hamilton mowed the Hessians down.

Rall received a bullet in his body, then two more in his side. He fell from his horse and was carried into a church. White handkerchiefs went up. Soon Washington accepted the surrender of 868 Hessians.

The general offered his sympathy to the dying Rall. "Treat my men with kindness," the Hessian colonel begged—and Washington promised. He was as good as his word. The disarmed men, whose prince had sold them to fight a people with whom they had no quarrel, were taken to Philadelphia. Later many of them settled in the West. Their children grew up as Americans, knowing what it was to be free men. The Hessians brought the Christmas tree to America. On it Washington hung the priceless gift of liberty.

The Continental Army took new heart after Trenton. When Washington, with the help of the Philadelphia banker Robert Morris, offered the men a bonus of ten dollars each, they agreed to serve for six weeks more.

The general was back in Trenton on New Year's Day. Across Assanpink Creek, east of the town, he formed his lines. The next day Cornwallis was marching down from Princeton with a mighty force. Sharp-shooters were posted in the woods to delay his coming. The fords and bridges at the creek were manned. But there were more redcoats than Washington had counted on—with still others on the way.

The campfires of the enemy armies blazed on opposite banks of the creek. Would the British attack that very night? Years later Washington heard what the tired Cornwallis said of him when he reached Assanpink Creek after a day of hard travel.

"I will bag the old fox in the morning," Cornwallis promised his officers.

But while Cornwallis slumbered Washington toiled. The night grew cold. The spongy ground froze hard. Rags were tied about the wagon wheels of the baggage train. It moved off silently. Men roused from sleep and formed in a shivering column. They moved north on the old Quaker Road. Again bare feet left prints of red upon the snow. A small guard was left behind to fool the foe across the creek.

"Pile the fence rails on the fire, my men, and never mind the noise," were the general's parting words to those who stayed behind. "Keep digging trenches, too, as if we meant to stay."

By morning the old fox was a dozen miles away.

A battle for breakfast was hard fare for men who had marched all night. But Washington's winter soldiers were growing used to it by now. Eight mornings ago they had whipped the Hessians. Now a back road was taking them into Princeton. More of the Cornwallis men were moving into this town.

A bold stroke now would smash this force and cut the enemy supply line from New York. There was no time to lose. This very moment Cornwallis must be cursing himself for letting the old fox go. He would try to make up for lost time now. Washington was between two British forces. The fox had better be quick or the jaws of the trap would shut on him.

The commander-in-chief sent General Mercer up Stony Creek to destroy the bridge over which the foe would try to cross. The sound of firing from an apple orchard by the Quaker meetinghouse told the commander that Mercer had met the enemy. Washington rallied troops to go to his aid. A regiment of redcoats had braved the volleys of the Americans. Now they were charging with bayonets.

It was hard to get green troops to stand against a moving line of bristling steel. Mercer was cut down while trying. Washington's men were wavering, too. The commander spurred his horse until he was in the line of cross fire.

"Parade with us, my brave fellow, there is but a handful of the enemy!" he called. The sight of the tall horseman moving through the bullets calmed his men. A line was thrown around the British, who were glad at last to break and flee. Some of them hid in Princeton College. While these were being flushed from Nassau Hall, Washington was off in pursuit of others.

"A fine fox hunt, my boys!" he cried. Now his heart beat strong with joy. How much better it was to be the hunter than the hunted!

North of Princeton the general paused for another council with his officers. Should they move on to New Brunswick and challenge Cornwallis himself? There were stocks of British goods in that city, besides a treasure chest of gold. But the men were too footsore to try it now.

Washington sighed. "With six hundred fresh troops on a forced march, we could seize New Brunswick and put an end to the war."

Instead the commander moved his weary army to Morristown. From winter quarters in this Jersey fastness he could watch Cornwallis and the Howes—making them fear to move far from New York.

After all, it was not a bad ten days' work for men with broken shoes and tattered shirts. Even the commander's garb of buff and blue was tied with string where the buttons were missing.

Lots of people were sorry now they had begged for the King's pardon. For New Jersey was American again.

Chapter 15: CAN SPRING BE FAR BEHIND?

WASHINGTON knew what he would do if he were in Howe's shoes. He would go up the Hudson and help Burgoyne, who was trying to take back Ticonderoga for the British. Then there would be a line of redcoats from New York to Canada.

The line would be there already, Washington knew, without the amazing zeal of the daring Arnold. With his tiny fleet on Lake Champlain Arnold had held the British up.

"Benedict Arnold is an active, judicious and brave officer," Washington remarked. " 'Tis a pity Congress passed him by in the promotions. I hope he will not take it too much to heart. The country has need of his ability."

The new aide-de-camp spoke up. "Sir, no man has more cause than you to be outdone with a blundering Congress. Yet in the face of a hundred disappointments, you never talk of resigning."

The pink-faced youth was Alexander Hamilton. He had made a name for himself at Trenton. Washington talked to him about the precious powder and other secret aid now coming in from France. Ben Franklin had arranged for it in Paris. Whether more help came depended on how well the Americans showed they could fight.

If only Washington could figure out what the sly, fat Howe had up his sleeve, he would know better how to prove his mettle to the French. When the British fleet weighed anchor at the end of May, was it to sail south or north?

Late in July two hundred ships appeared in the mouth of the Delaware. It looked as though Howe intended to capture Philadelphia. Washington hurried to the defense, only to see Howe's fleet disappear again. Perhaps the wily Briton was only fooling and would go up the Hudson after all. For Burgoyne was cutting south through the forests. Already Ticonderoga had fallen. Washington wished that Arnold could defend the Hudson, but Congress put General Gates in command instead.

During that anxious August another youth came to Washington's camp near Philadelphia. He was French and of noble birth. He was called the Marquis de Lafayette. Lafayette was only nineteen when he heard of General Washington's crusade for freedom —and made up his mind to join him. Leaving his native land he told his friends, "The welfare of America is the welfare of mankind."

Now he stood before his hero, face radiant with idealism. "The moment I heard of America I loved her," he told the general.

"You will not find here the luxuries you are used to at court," replied Washington.

"I am here to learn, not to teach," said the youth.

In a gesture of affection the commander laid a hand on Lafayette's shoulder.

On August 22nd the enemy fleet appeared in Chesapeake Bay. It was headed for the Maryland shore, fifty miles south of Philadelphia. Washington was glad to see Howe so far away from the Hudson.

"Now let all New England turn out and crush Burgoyne!" he cried.

But Philadelphia had reason for alarm. To give the people courage, Washington paraded his army through the streets. Lafayette rode by his side. The columns of the army had grown longer. The men marched with a brave step to the sound of fife and drum. The army had a flag now, for Congress had added a field of thirteen stars to the banner with stripes of red and white. The men still did not have a uniform, however. They counted themselves lucky to have clothes at all.

In just one way they looked alike. Each soldier wore jauntily in his hat a twig of greenery.

Washington had to lead his army south and try to steer the redcoats away from Philadelphia. He took his stand at a ford where the Brandywine becomes a torrent between two cliffs. This was where Howe would try to cross. Could Washington stop him?

On the morning of September 11th his men traded fire with the Hessians on the other bank. Confused stories came in that Howe himself was crossing the Brandywine higher upstream in order to get behind the Americans and fire on them from both sides. When this was finally found to be true, General Sullivan swung into line against him. Lafayette begged for a part in the dangerous assignment and went with him. But it was too late to stem the British. The American line was broken and forced back. The brave Frenchman received a musket ball in his left leg, but hardly noticed it in the heat of battle.

"You have a bootful of blood," someone told him later. Lafayette considered the wound a decoration. It was an honor to bleed for American liberty.

Washington told the surgeon, "Treat him as if he were my son, for I love him as if he were."

Rain ruined the powder. Before the commander-in-chief could make another stand, the British were across the Schuylkill. On the 26th, Howe was in Germantown. Cornwallis was marching into Philadelphia, his band playing "God Save the King."

Washington, deeply disappointed, planned a counterblow. He would make it hot for Howe in Germantown.

By night, early in October, he sent columns into the town by four roads. The Americans were to come together in the market place, sweeping the British before them as into a sheepfold.

It looked that morning as though the bold stroke would succeed. The enemy resisted at every wall and hedge, but bayonets crowded them back. The attackers tore into the paper cartridges with their teeth till their lips were black. They rammed the charges into the muskets. A fog made the powder stream down their cheeks. It grew so murky that friend could not be told from foe.

By now the redcoats were surrendering. A few of them made a fortress of a big stone house. Wayne's men tried to blast them out. They ran into another force in the fog. For a while Americans were firing upon Americans.

The victory tide began to ebb. At length all Washington could do was to take away his army in good order. It was no victory. But at least his men had shown the world they were not afraid to fight.

Late that month better news than Washington dared hope for came from the North. Burgoyne had not realized how big America was. The British general did not know what Washington had learned twenty years before . . . how hard it is to find wagons, hay and food in a wilderness. Sharpshooters hid behind trees—picking off his men on the lonely trails. His retreat to Canada was cut off. Arnold, in a frenzy of action, rallied the Americans wherever they faltered.

And now at Saratoga Burgoyne had surrendered to Gates with nearly ten thousand men!

Washington's voice choked with emotion as he read the message. It did not seem to matter that—when the greatest battle of the war was won—another general commanded. Only America's freedom mattered.

The quarters of the Continental Army that winter were at Valley Forge. The ridges overlooking the Schuylkill here, a score of miles from Philadelphia, were well fortified. There was a house for Washington on this bleak hillside. However, he kept to his army tent, sharing the hardships of his men while they were putting up the rows of square log huts.

The comfort-loving Howe had a mansion in Phila-delphia. His life was a gay round in a brilliant society. The Loyalists were having their inning now. Congress, pushed from Independence Hall, had moved to cramped quarters in York, Pennsylvania. Its members were edgy. While Gates was winning a great victory at Saratoga, Washington had made them move from Philadelphia.

There was talk of putting Gates in Washington's place. The anti-Washington clique even tried to win away the loyal Lafayette. At a dinner the young man was seated at the right of General Gates. Toasts were offered to the new hero, to Congress, to France—to everyone but General Washington. When it was La-fayette's turn, however, he raised his glass high and cried, "The commander-in-chief of the armies of the United States!" He had made clear his loyalty.

All this time the commander had an army to feed and clothe. Congress had sent all too few supplies to him. Its paper Continental dollars were falling fast. Why should the farmers give up good grain and meat for worthless paper?

Christmas came—a year since the raid on Trenton had turned the tide. Yet in some ways things were even blacker now. There was not a cow to kill for meat in all the camp. There were only twenty-five barrels of flour to feed an entire army.

It was freezing cold in Valley Forge in January and

February. Bare feet in the snow were nothing new in Washington's army. This winter even blankets were hard to find. Men sat all night around log fires—rubbing their hands and losing sleep.

Every horse was a bag of bones for lack of forage. Starving men twisted grapevines into harnesses for one another. While one man pulled the sled, another searched the countryside for food.

In February two welcome visitors came to share the hardships of Valley Forge. One was Mrs. Washington. The ladies of the neighborhood put on their best dresses to visit Lady Washington. They met a woman in a simple house dress, her hazel eyes intent on her chores. She was knitting socks, making shirts and mending trousers. They heard how she visited dying men and prayed with them.

The other visitor was General Steuben. This gruff Prussian had been on the staff of Frederick the Great. Now, like the Poles, Pulaski and Kosciusko—and more Frenchmen all the time—he was in America to fight for freedom.

Steuben was made inspector general of the army, for he was a famous drillmaster. He didn't know much English. His orders were mixed with French and German as he taught the ragged men to keep in step and obey commands. Sometimes he quite lost patience with their awkwardness and called an American officer to his side.

"Here, you swear at them in English," he would cry. And the men grew fond of Steuben, for he was turning them into soldiers.

Washington made General Greene his quartermaster. Supplies began to flow into camp. As the ground thawed so did the spirits of the army. The younger officers formed a dinner club. No one without holes in his breeches could join. It was their little joke.

The men in the ranks had their jests, too. They draped their winter blankets about their shoulders and paraded. "Look at our new spring coats," they shouted. A game called "bases" became popular. Washington was among those who found fun in this early form of baseball.

The trees were green and the meadows gay with flowers when a courier burst into camp with happy news. In Paris Ben Franklin had signed a treaty of alliance with the King of France. America would no longer fight alone against the British Empire. Two events had taught the French that the Americans had real staying power. One was Burgoyne's surrender at Saratoga. The other was Washington's brave attack at Germantown.

The commander-in-chief heard the news with solemn joy. The young Lafayette broke into tears. He threw his arms about Washington. He kissed his general on both cheeks.

Chapter 16: THE WORLD TURNED UPSIDE DOWN

THE MOSQUITOES sang and stung. The soldiers reeled under their packs in the stifling heat. The blankets they longed for at Valley Forge seemed to mock them on the hot Jersey sands.

Under the lash of Washington's restless energy the march continued. Just beyond, fifteen hundred wagons loaded with British war supplies were threading their way in a slender column. The rich prize was in the care of General Clinton. He was taking the place of Howe, who had gone home.

Washington was in hot pursuit. He saw a chance

to scatter an army, seize an arsenal—and feed and clothe his needy men.

Lafayette went out with three detachments to attack the rear of the army. General Charles Lee had turned the mission down. He was back—after a trade of prisoners. He could not believe the Americans had learned to fight while he was away.

Then Lee thought of the glory he might lose. He told Washington he had decided to go after all.

This was embarrassing, but Lafayette took no offense. He put himself under Lee as a volunteer. As soon as the British moved off from Monmouth Courthouse in the morning, Lee was to strike the enemy rear. Washington, with the main army, would then close in.

At the sound of musketry and cannon after daybreak, Washington quickened the step of his columns. They came to a bridge over a deep ravine. There signs of trouble began to appear. Stragglers came in with stories of retreat. Soon whole regiments were streaming back, uncertain of their orders. They were fleeing from the redcoats. That is all they knew.

Washington acted quickly. He ordered the artillery to a near-by orchard. The brave Wayne—Mad Anthony he was called—was told to guard the bridge. Lines were formed on the high ground behind, one under Lafayette's command.

The last to appear was the distraught Lee.

"What is the meaning, sir, of this retreat?" Washington demanded.

Lee stammered something about confusion he could not control and orders that were not obeyed. He had doubted if the attack could succeed.

"You should never have undertaken what you did not mean to carry through." And Washington stormed at the cowardly Lee until the leaves on the trees seemed to shake.

The Battle of Monmouth raged all afternoon—with Washington in command. By now Clinton had wheeled about with his best fighting men. Wayne's Pennsylvania line held the bridge against soldiers who were the pride of Europe. Greene commanded the right wing. When the left began to crumble, Steuben was there—barking out orders. The men were disciplined now. They formed their line again.

Many who were not struck by bullets died of the heat that day. A fine white horse dropped under Washington. He leaped into the saddle of a chestnut mare and was off among the bullets, giving his commands. Clinton was unable to crack the line. He left the battlefield to the Americans. He had lost an engagement to men who no longer ran . . . at least when Washington was around. But Clinton saved his fifteen hundred wagons.

Washington and Lafayette lay under a cloak at the foot of a tree. There they talked the night away.

Their conversation was of the faithless Lee and of the treasure caravan he had let slip through his fingers.

In the fall of 1780 Washington was riding on a secret journey to Hartford, Connecticut. A score of dragoons was his guard. Lafayette and Hamilton were at his side. He was about to meet General Rochambeau and Admiral de Ternay, who came to America in the name of the King of France.

The night before he had dined at West Point with General Arnold. It was good to feel that this strong point, guarding the lifeline of the Hudson, was in trustworthy hands.

Yet Washington was sad. The fruits of the long war were few indeed—measured against the high hopes of two years ago.

Could worse luck possibly have befallen the French fleet? First it was unable to pass the shallow channel of New York Harbor, then it was tossed by a storm off Newport, Rhode Island . . . sent to Boston for repairs . . . called away to the West Indies. Now after two long years another fleet was at Newport. Would luck be any better this time?

The worst of it was that Washington's countrymen now expected the French to win the war for them. He had been shocked, on visiting Philadelphia, to see luxury on every side, while his poor soldiers were unpaid.

143

By now Congress was almost too weak to matter. Washington was forced to appeal to each separate state for men and clothes.

"A wagonload of paper money will scarcely purchase a wagonload of supplies," said Washington thoughtfully to himself. He reached into a pocket of his long blue coat and jingled some coins. The epaulettes on the shoulders of the coat marked him as commander-in-chief. But the hard money in the pocket was a loan from friends to pay for his lodging.

Well, it was nothing to the loan he would ask of his French allies . . . not for himself but to save his country.

The redcoats were overrunning the Southland now. Georgia was in British hands. Gates, the hero of Saratoga, had lost an army at Camden, South Carolina. The road to Virginia was open.

The commander-in-chief was like a caged tiger. The bars of his cage were the Hudson and the Delaware rivers. He had to pace this narrow cage, helpless to defend the South, yet too weak to drive Clinton from New York.

These were Washington's melancholy thoughts as he traveled the road to Hartford.

The high French officers admired this majestic, sad and gentle man whose deeds were stirring Europe. They agreed it would be a fine idea to storm New York by land and sea. Unfortunately, they added, one could only wait. Half their fleet was bottled up in Brest, France. The British were hovering outside Newport, waiting for a chance to attack the other half. All they could do was ask their King for more ships, more men, more money.

Would the need for patience never end? On the way back to West Point Washington tried to find some ground for cheer. He thought of John Paul Jones, the fearless privateer, who was boarding British ships and had even sunk a man-of-war off Scotland.

And think of George Rogers Clark. Washington's friends—Thomas Jefferson, Patrick Henry and George Mason—had sent him into the West with a tiny band of men. He had won an empire that stretched to the Mississippi.

The commander-in-chief sent Hamilton ahead to tell Arnold of his coming. He was in a mood for a hearty breakfast. The aide found Arnold pacing nervously, a letter in his hand. He must hurry to the garrison, he told Hamilton, and would be back at once. The commander grew annoyed as the morning passed. This was a rude way to treat a guest.

Then a package came for General Washington. A letter explained that its contents had been found on Major André, a captured British spy. Here were the plans of West Point, the location of its guns, the size of its garrison—all an enemy would want to know before attacking. And they were in the handwriting of Benedict Arnold!

Washington sank limply into a chair. He passed the papers to Lafayette. He buried his head in his hands.

"Arnold has betrayed us! Whom can we trust now?" he groaned.

It was six years since George Washington had seen Mount Vernon. Even now he could pause but briefly. Mrs. Washington and all the household were in a mighty bustle. Company was coming, important company—General Rochambeau and other famous Frenchmen. They had paid General Washington the honors due a marshal of France. Mount Vernon should not fail in returning hospitality.

Washington took a quick look at his estate. Some things a man must do himself if he wants them done right. On the whole, however, Cousin Lund Washington had been a faithful manager. Once, indeed, he had been too cautious. When British vessels appeared off Mount Vernon, Cousin Lund had carried out food and refreshments to put the officers in good humor. General Washington grew quite angry on hearing of this. Better the house be burned and his plantation laid in ruins than buy off the British!

More than once the general's patience had snapped —waiting, always waiting, for the chance to attack New York that never came. He had even quarreled with Hamilton. After hot words his proud aide had gone off to seek military honors in the field. So now he had a new aide—his stepson, Jacky Custis. Why was the general's temper so bad? Maybe it was because of those teeth that plagued him so! They had bothered him for many years. Now his real ones had quite decayed and he had false teeth carved of ivory. They were more for looks than use. As long as he kept his jaws shut tight, a metal spring held them in place. Sitting for his portrait, however, he looked a little grim. But the French insisted on having his picture.

Now, in 1781 they were proving good allies. An army of two nations was on the march to strike a blow together—not against New York but in Virginia. As they stepped onto boats in Maryland, Washington's men wore French clothes, carried French guns and had French money in their pockets.

How much had happened in the South since Washington sent Lafayette to punish the traitor Arnold! A British general now, Arnold took delight in plundering former friends. Pillars of smoke marked his party's path as they raided through Virginia. The air was thick with tobacco smoke from burning warehouses and the pitch and resin of boats in flame.

Washington would give his teeth all over again to capture the man he most abhorred. But Arnold got away.

Lafayette was shadowing Cornwallis across Virginia now, watching him like a hawk from the opposite bank of the York River, crossing to attack with his weak force whenever he dared.

For Cornwallis was losing the lower South. "Whom can we trust now?" Washington had asked, after Arnold turned to treason. His answer was Nathanael Greene, the old blacksmith, who took command in the Carolinas at the darkest hour.

"We fight, get beat, rise and fight again," Greene wrote to Washington. He linked his campaign with the raids of farmers and frontiersmen. These partisan bands struck sudden blows at the British, then disappeared into the swamps. At length the blacksmith and his helpers were beating out an anvil chorus. A victory on Kings Mountain was followed by one at Cowpens, where Morgan's riflemen won deathless glory. After the Battle of Guilford Courthouse Cornwallis moved toward the Virginia coast at Yorktown.

Now Washington and Rochambeau hurried from the merrymaking at Mount Vernon, hoping to hem in Cornwallis. Admiral de Grasse, with a French fleet, was guarding the bay. Washington visited his flagship late in September.

"My dear little General," the French admiral exclaimed, kissing Washington on both cheeks. And everybody laughed because, although de Grasse was tall, he was not as tall as Washington. But he was in a gay mood, for he had just beaten off an attacking British fleet. Besides, France had new friends. Spain and Holland were fighting Britain, too.

Cornwallis had his back to the sea, waiting for help that never came. He turned the town into a fortress. But Washington had built a trap around him. Now he began to spring the trap.

The French on the left and the Americans on the right formed a half-moon around Yorktown, each horn resting on the river. Siege guns went into action on October 6th. The first rim of the British defense was taken. The allies were six hundred yards from the town's center now.

Ceaseless cannon fire knocked out the batteries of Cornwallis, one by one. He lost his second defense rim on October 12th. Two British dugouts were stormed in the night—one by the French, the other by Americans under Lafayette.

Cornwallis sent raiders out to spike the big guns. But they were soon back in repair. He tried to get his troops out on boats at night, but a storm drove them in again.

On the 17th a British officer stepped to a parapet with a white flag and beat a drum. Cornwallis was ready to arrange the terms of surrender. Washington ordered the firing to cease.

The following afternoon the American troops under Washington—and the French under Rochambeau—formed in facing lines in front of the post at Yorktown. Cornwallis was too ill to come. He sent his sword by an officer who tried to deliver it to Rochambeau. The redcoats would rather give up to the French than to rebels!

But Rochambeau made it plain that it was Washington who commanded here. An American officer took the sword. The generous Washington sent it back to Cornwallis to keep.

The defeated garrison marched out, its flags furled, its band playing an old British march. The tune was called "The World Turned Upside Down."

Proud Cornwallis was surrendering eight thousand redcoats to a rebel general. It was the world turned upside down all right!

When Cornwallis felt better he was the guest of Washington and Rochambeau at dinner. Here he complimented Washington for the siege of Yorktown and, above all, for his great skill at Trenton and Princeton five years before.

Toasts were offered to the King of France and to the Continental Army. There was an awkward pause when Cornwallis proposed the health of "His Majesty."

Washington rose to the occasion.

"Yes, to the King of England," he said. "And may he always stay over there."

Chapter *17:* BACK TO THE FARM

THE NATION celebrated Yorktown's surrender with
fireworks and bells. But Washington was sad as he
hurried to Williamsburg. His aide and stepson Jacky
Custis had come down with camp fever. He was
barely able to stand when Cornwallis' men laid down
their arms. Now he was dying.

Jacky's mother and his weeping wife were at the
bedside as the end came. Mrs. Washington, gray with
many cares, now had lost both her children. The
young widow, still a girl, was left with four.

Washington knew he must arrange the funeral and
stay home a little while to comfort the family.

He stayed just long enough for his heart to come under siege . . . and to surrender to two babies.

George Washington Parke Custis—what a big name for a tiny infant, who stared wide eyed from his cradle at his step-grandpapa!

And Nelly with her dark eyes and ringlets. She was two. She put her little hand in his with trust. There was not a trace of fear as she joined him on his walks.

The Father of his Country, they called him now . . . the man who had no children of his own.

Washington had to hasten north to join his army. Before he left he said to Martha, "Let us adopt the two littlest ones to be the joy of our later years."

Back on the Hudson Washington waited out the weary months. The redcoats were still in New York. England was too weak to make war but too proud to make peace. The Continental Army was too weak to drive the redcoats out. Who wanted to join an army when payday never came?

The officers were grumbling, too. They had given their best years to their country. It looked as though an ungrateful nation would leave them to an old age of poverty.

One spring day a letter came to the commander-in-chief from a Colonel Nicola. He wrote in the name of a group of officers. They despaired, he said, of getting justice from a weak republic. Washington had the talents to command an army. Let him use these same talents, they asked, to lead the nation as a King.

Nothing since the war began shocked Washington so much as this. Now he began to understand why a weak Congress had always feared a strong army.

Well, he would make it clear where he stood. The man who would not be a King summoned two aides as witnesses. Then he replied to Nicola. "If you have any regard for your country, or respect for me, banish these thoughts from your mind," he wrote. Off went the letter. A copy was signed by the witnesses. The general sealed it, his face grim. The copy went into the army's records. Now let anyone, in time to come, say that Washington ever wanted to be a King!

By fall England, at last, was ready to recognize American independence. Peace terms were being worked out in Paris. Martha begged him to come home for the winter. But Washington could not leave. It would be his eighth winter with the army. Without him at the camp there would be trouble.

"We have guns in our hands," the soldiers were saying. "If the country will not give us justice, we will take it."

A meeting of officers was called in March. Some of them wanted the army to set up a dictator. If Washington opposed the idea they would throw him out!

The commander-in-chief was on hand, troubled

but knowing his duty. He fumbled in his pockets for his glasses and his notes as he rose to speak.

"Gentlemen, you will permit me to put on my spectacles, for I have not only grown gray, but almost blind, in the service of my country," he said.

Washington was fifty-one. He looked older. Tears came to the eyes of his comrades in battle as the man who had led them through so many troubles promised not to rest until he had got them justice. Two months later Congress voted back pay to the army. By that time peace had come. Before the end of the year the redcoats had left New York.

It was December. At last Washington could go home, his duty done. He sat with his officers at Fraunces Tavern in New York. Some of them had been at his side in the siege of Boston, nearly nine years ago. Others crossed the icy Delaware on Christmas night—or shared the hardships of Valley Forge. This was the last time they would meet together.

When the time for parting came, Washington said, "With a heart full of love and gratitude, I now take leave of you. I most devoutly wish that your latter days may be as prosperous as your former ones have been glorious and honorable." Then he added, "I shall be obliged to you if each will come and take me by the hand."

The gray eyes of the commander were moist as he

grasped each hand in turn. It was not often his way to be emotional, but now he kissed each man on the cheek in the French fashion.

These were the brave men who had led the Revolution. There was not a dry eye as Washington left the tavern and stepped onto a barge that would take him across the Hudson.

The journey southward was halted at Annapolis for a meeting with Congress. Here he became Mr. Washington again. He had received his commission from Congress. Now he was giving it up to Congress. It was a weak body. Often he had complained of its slowness. But it was the voice of the nation. Someday, perhaps, it would be stronger.

Mrs. Washington was with him on the homeward lap. The tired soldier leaned toward her. "Now I can return to the country and end my days in quiet."

He was silent awhile. Then a pleasant thought softened the tired lines.

"If we hurry," he said, "we can be home by Christmas Eve."

The master's homecoming was the signal for Mount Vernon's merriest Christmas. Washington and Custis kin were on hand to welcome the couple on that frosty eve. There was dancing in the mansion house and in the slave quarters, too. For this was the season when even the slaves were permitted many liberties. How beautiful their melodies sounded on the cold night air! What a racket the fireworks made! On every cove of Dogue Run and Little Hunting Creek a bonfire was blazing.

Cries of "Christmas Gift!" were heard next morning. This was the greeting of the house servants. They hoped to be given a copper coin. There were children to shout the greeting now, too, for Nelly was four and little Washington two.

People came from miles around to honor their great neighbor. The dinner table was piled high with turkey and ham and apple and pumpkin pies. But the thing you saw first, right in the center of the table, was a suckling pig with an apple in its mouth. And after dinner Washington could linger and munch nuts to his heart's content. For there were no letters to write to Congress about the army's needs.

Washington wrote his good friend Lafayette, "I have retired from public employments and will move gently down the stream of life until I sleep with my fathers."

It had been painful to part from the youth who was like a son. As their carriages separated, Washington wondered whether it was the last time he would ever see Lafayette. He wanted to answer, No. But his fears answered, Yes.

The two men exchanged letters and gifts across

the sea. Washington was out at dawn with French hunting dogs Lafayette had sent him. He received many gifts, for the name of Washington was famous in every land.

Hearing that Washington wanted to improve the breed of mules, the King of Spain sent a handsome jackass to Mount Vernon. The noble animal was called Royal Gift. A servant was proud to take him on a tour of the countryside, shouting as he went, "Make way for the jackass of the King of Spain!" People poured out to stare at Royal Gift, not because he once belonged to the King of Spain but because he now belonged to George Washington.

An endless stream of visitors came to Mount Vernon as to a shrine. Painters and sculptors wanted to record Washington's likeness for future ages. There were nephews and nieces by the dozen, all finding their place in their uncle's heart. He was soon paying for the schooling of a number of them.

Once in a while Washington complained that his home was like "a well-resorted tavern." How pleasant it was one June evening in 1785 to dine alone with Mrs. Washington!

"Martha," he remarked, "this is the first time since my retirement that we have been by ourselves."

Washington was a busy farmer again. Walls and fences were in bad repair. There was an icehouse to build under the banquet hall. A winding drive made a fine approach to the mansion. Deer, grazing on the grass, kept it cropped. New paving stones were laid on the piazza with its majestic view of the Potomac.

Standing there as evening gathered, Washington's gaze swept the broad river. But his mind roamed beyond the Potomac to the Ohio and the Mississippi. Before long he was on a trip to the western lands, straightening out his old claims with the new nation.

There was much talk now of a new kind of boat that would work by steam. What a blessing it would be for traveling on these western waters! Soon Washington had a part in a plan to build canals and link the James and Potomac rivers with the Ohio.

"My first wish is to see war banished from the earth," he wrote. "Let the oppressed of the earth and those who want land come to our western country and dwell in peace."

Waterways, linking East and West, would knit the nation together where Congress failed, he felt. He rode to Alexandria for a meeting of Virginia and Maryland men to talk about boat travel on the Potomac. Soon he had invited them all to Mount Vernon. Washington didn't know it yet, but he was back in public life.

Chapter 18: THE NEW ROOF

IT WAS a chill spring day. Washington's rheumatism bothered him. What in the world had ever made him leave comfortable Mount Vernon for the tiring journey to Philadelphia. If he had let other people worry about the country for a change, he wouldn't have to go to this Constitutional Convention.

Washington remembered how he had poured out his feelings to the earnest James Madison about the state of the nation. It cost so much blood and treasure to get the country going. Now it was drifting apart, he feared.

One state wouldn't accept another's money. It

wouldn't even accept its own. The farmers were in debt and ready to riot because stores and banks wouldn't take their paper money and mark their bills paid.

The United States could get no more loans in Europe. "You are one country when you borrow money," the Europeans said. "You are thirteen independent states when we ask you to pay it back."

Waterways, connecting one state with another, were badly needed. Even on dry land the flow of goods from state to state was blocked. You often had to pay a tariff to move your merchandise across the line.

Madison took these complaints to heart. He saw to it that Virginia sent delegates to help write a better Constitution. He put Washington's name at the head of the list. Washington had vowed he was through with public life. And here he was—riding into Philadelphia. Soldiers were cutting a path for him through cheering crowds.

At Independence Hall Robert Morris suggested George Washington for chairman. Before he knew it, Washington was sitting in a chair up in front . . . a big chair with armrests and a back decorated with the upper half of a gilded sun.

Washington sat there day after day. Weeks went by. He seldom spoke. But he listened well. He was friends once more with his wartime aide. Alexander Hamilton was now a brilliant orator.

"The British government is the best in the world," young Hamilton declared. "I doubt whether anything short of it will do in America."

But America was just rid of monarchy. The nation was in no mood to try anything like that again. Even a strong federal government, as Madison wanted, was held in fear. The most that people would stand for, it was said, was giving Congress a little more power.

Washington rose from the chair to make one of his few speeches. "If, to please the people, we offer what we ourselves disapprove, how can we afterward defend our work?" he asked.

All through the hot summer they argued . . . the men who were to be called the Founding Fathers. In September they had a Constitution ready. It did not please anyone too much, but it was the best they could agree on at all. Old Benjamin Franklin's face was wreathed in smiles. He gazed for the last time at the half-sun on Washington's chair. Franklin was over eighty now. "As I have been sitting here all these weeks," he said in a quavering voice, "I have often wondered whether yonder sun is rising or setting. Now I know that it is a rising sun."

The sun still had to climb from the horizon to the zenith. How would the thirteen states take to the new Constitution? Would they vote to accept it?

Would they hand over part of their powers to a federal government?

Washington had been away four months and fourteen days. Back at Mount Vernon he wrote letters asking his many friends to support the new Constitution.

"I sincerely believe it is the best that can be obtained at this time," he told Patrick Henry. "The door is open for amendment later."

But many did not like the new Constitution—and Henry was among them. The self-reliant farmers from whom he sprang feared the rule of a strong and distant hand. A hand reaching into their pockets for taxes was not a welcome hand, whether it moved from London or Philadelphia. What did it matter if money was hard to borrow in Europe? A gun would supply their needs for game. An ax would make a clearing in the forest.

How could the new Congress represent the people, others asked, when so many of the people had no property and couldn't vote?

So it was uphill work passing the new Constitution. Having come this far, however, Washington wouldn't give up.

Thomas Jefferson wanted a Bill of Rights added to the Constitution, so Americans would always have free speech, religious liberty and trial by jury.

Debate was hot and heavy over the New Roof.

This was what they were calling the Constitution now . . . a New Roof for the nation. Finally friends told Washington that the New Roof would win. People were willing to trust it for shelter because word was around that Washington would be the first President of the United States.

So in April, 1789, Washington was on the road again, this time to New York. He was sorrier than ever that he had meddled in politics.

"I feel like a culprit going to the place of execution." These were his mournful words.

Why had he accepted the presidency? It was because of those letters from Alexander Hamilton. Hamilton insisted that the Father of his Country must give the Constitution a chance to work. "No other man," he warned, "can unite public opinion during the first years of the new government."

No one was as popular as Washington. That was sure. Everyone was turning out to cheer the President-elect. An escort welcomed him at every town. The streets were gay with flags and flowers. In village after village they put the old general on a dapper white horse and paraded him down Main Street. The man who loved horses so much grew weary of them on this trip . . . especially white horses.

When Washington crossed the Delaware this time, he entered Trenton under a triumphal arch. Maidens robed in white and scattering blossoms made a path through the yelling throngs. "Strew the hero's way with flowers," they chanted.

Washington was too worn out to enjoy it much. He dreaded the task that lay ahead. When I am through being President and travel the other way, will they cheer me then? he wondered.

New York was to be the capital for a time. The biggest celebration of all was here. Cannons boomed as the barge crossed the river. Bands blared and thousands shouted themselves hoarse.

As Washington stepped onto the red carpet that was rolled down to the waterside, welcoming hands guided him toward a splendid coach. Six horses were to draw him through the multitude to his house on Cherry Street . . . six white horses!

The President-elect scowled at the sight of them. Ridiculous! It was only a short walk to his house. So, with troops making way, he strode off on foot, his lips pressed tight over the teeth he wore for company.

The head of the new government could not escape the coach-and-six on Inauguration Day. This stately carriage, decorated with cherubs, was a sort of new roof for Washington. It shut him off from the open skies. It was a sign of the ceremony he must endure.

Officers in bright uniforms headed the procession to Federal Hall. Washington met John Adams in the

Senate Chamber. Adams was to be Vice-President. Right now he was as fidgety as could be, wondering if this was the way they would do things in London.

The eyes of the crowd outside were on the balcony. Washington, pale and gaunt, appeared there to take the oath of office. He was a noble figure in a dark brown suit, stiff in the joints but standing erect. His white hair was powdered. His dress sword hung in a white scabbard at his side.

Washington was asked to swear faithfully to perform the duties of his high office. "I do, so help me God," he promised. His hand lay on a Bible as he spoke the solemn words . . . a big hand on a big Bible.

Back in the Senate Chamber the hand trembled as the man who had never flinched at bullets read his speech. His voice was weak. The congressmen strained to hear. After it was over, the President of the United States knew that one thing, at least, had been done right. The dark brown suit he wore came from Hartford, Connecticut. It was of American make.

Mrs. Washington came with the children in May to be the First Lady of the Land. Never was the President so glad to see his family. With them he could be natural. He was hemmed in on every hand. He couldn't call on an old friend, as this would make others jealous. They must visit him instead—and then so many came he couldn't do his work. So now he could only receive important people—and on a certain day.

Brows were wrinkled over what to call him. Should it be Your Excellency? Your High Mightiness? Or, perhaps, Your Elective Majesty? They couldn't agree on a high-sounding title. So Washington became plain Mr. President. That was all right with him.

Washington looked forward to the first presidential ball. He was not too old to dance a step or two. But when he did, however, there were disapproving whispers in his ear. The President must not dance. His duty was to stand while others danced . . . and just look dignified.

Back home, among good friends, he could be quite merry. Now, at formal dinners, he was as solemn as an owl. The President had his receptions on Tuesday afternoons. He stood in front of the fireplace, bowing to each guest in turn. His sword was buckled on. In his hand he held a hat with an ostrich feather. He did not need a free hand to offer friends. It would not be dignified for a president to shake hands, they said.

It was like a court. Tongues wagged over all this stiff bowing, as if Washington were to blame for it. The President grew a little irritated. If his bows were stiff, he said, it was due to age and not to pride of office.

How he longed for the life of a farmer! The only pleasure he found was at the theater. For a while he was deathly ill with a tumor in his leg. News came from Fredericksburg of his mother's passing . . . the mother who thought of him all his life as her rash boy, heedless of redskins and redcoats and the stormy sea.

Letters from Lafayette told of France's taking the path of liberty where America had blazed a way. A key came, too. Once this key had turned the lock on the prison doors of the Bastille, as they shut on freedom-loving Frenchmen. Ten weeks after Washington became President the Bastille fell in France's glorious Revolution. Now this key was a Key of Freedom. Lafayette said it belonged to Washington more than to any other man.

The President of the United States fingered the key fondly. Someday his duty would be done. Then he would unlock the doors of his own prison house and rest once more under the old roof at Mount Vernon.

Chapter *19:* TWO PARTIES

No OTHER MAN could unite the nation. This was
what Hamilton said of Washington. Could even
Washington unite it and keep it so?

As 1790 passed, his hopes were high. The United
States now had more than four million people, the
census showed. Surely it was worth while for all men
to work together for the happiness of their growing
country.

The capital had moved to Philadelphia. The President and his family were in the handsome brick mansion of Robert Morris.

There had been a few hard words over those certificates Washington's army got in place of pay. The new federal government was to guarantee them, a hundred cents on the dollar. The trouble was the news leaked out too soon. Greedy men set out on sailing vessels and fast horses to buy up the certificates cheap. All too often they reaped the profit—instead of the old soldiers.

Washington was grieved to hear of this. Hamilton called it an accident that couldn't be helped. The most important thing, he said, was to prove that the credit of the new government was good.

Alexander Hamilton was Washington's Secretary of the Treasury now. He had a boy's face and a giant's brain. He dreamed of an America where able men might grow wealthy on the trade and manufactures of a spreading continent.

Thomas Jefferson was Secretary of State. He was the chief writer of the Declaration of Independence, which said that all men were created equal. He had seen another revolution for the rights of man in France. A country without rich or poor, where every man might own a shop or farm—this was what he wanted America to be.

What a contrast in these two men . . . the stubby, restless Hamilton . . . loose-jointed Jefferson, buried in thought. Washington needed them both in his Cabinet, working together "to form a more perfect Union," as it said in the Constitution.

Laws to help manufacturers were linking the owners of factories to the federal government. Merchants and bankers were happy to see it take over the old debts of the states. These were northern interests, but there was something to please the South too. A new capital for the nation was to rise on the banks of the Potomac.

Washington busied himself with Indian affairs, smoking the pipe of peace with chieftains who called in friendship at the Morris House—sending his own warriors against those who took up the hatchet. He traveled through New England and the South. For he wanted to see all of the United States with his own eyes. Soon, with Vermont and Kentucky, there would be fifteen of them.

The President inspected the site of the new capital with particular pleasure. It was across from Alexandria and not far from Mount Vernon. A famous Frenchman Major L'Enfant was planning a city with circles and broad avenues that led out from the center like the spokes of a wheel.

This was to be called the city of Washington. But Washington would always call it the Federal City.

"The public buildings," he suggested, "should look beyond the present day."

By the vote of all the electors, Washington was called to the presidency for a second term. He was told he must stay at the helm a little longer until the ship was clear of shoals and banks.

Signs of party strife began to appear before the election was over. If Hamilton was the fair-haired boy of the well born, Jefferson was the idol of the mechanics and humble farmers. How much longer could this high-spirited pair stay hitched together? Not long, it seemed. In 1793 a new representative came from Paris—the fiery Genêt. Citizen Genêt he was called, for he did not come in the King's name but as a citizen of Revolutionary France. The King was dead. "Long live the people," was now the cry.

At Charleston, where Genêt came ashore, American citizens put on French liberty caps and danced in the streets to welcome him. All the way to Philadelphia he met friends of France. Washington feared the friendly welcome was going to the envoy's head. Genêt, he heard, was making plans for privateers to sail from American ports and capture English vessels. The Frenchman claimed this was only right under the treaty by which France stood by America's side at Yorktown.

When Washington's Cabinet met, Hamilton lashed out against the new France. He said the treaty was only with the French king. Jefferson, though he could not excuse the behavior of Genêt, was more than ever a friend of France's freedom-loving people. The President made up his mind while the two men clashed. The United States was a new nation, struggling to live. It must not spend its strength on foreign wars. In the quarrel between England and France it must take neither side.

When Genêt called on Washington the President was chilly. The caller left in a huff. An old picture of the King of France was looking down on him from the President's wall. This inflamed his spirits all the more. The flame could not be quenched. Genêt appealed to the American people over the head of their president. Soon the country was in a furore.

At length the rash Genêt fitted out a privateer in Philadelphia Harbor. The ship sailed away before it could be stopped. Jefferson had to ask Genêt to go back to France for disobeying the President's order.

Cabinet meetings became ordeals to the President. To both Hamilton and Jefferson he put a question. "Why can you make no allowance for the opinions of the other?" he asked.

How could they? To Hamilton, his rival was arousing the mob against men who were the backbone of the nation. Jefferson blamed Hamilton for using power in the President's name to enrich the few.

An overshadowing horror brought a brief truce in the summer of 1793. An enemy that knew no politics was stealing into Philadelphia from wharves and frog ponds fringing the city. It was the scourge of yellow fever. Death-wagons rumbled through the streets, carrying thousands to the burying ground.

Because his advisers insisted, the President and his family went to Mount Vernon. Hamilton and Jefferson stayed at their posts. The fever laid the Secretary of the Treasury low and he nearly died. The Secretary of State was spared to guide the nation's troubled foreign affairs.

The parting of the ways came after frost drove out the yellow plague. Jefferson told the sorrowing President he could serve his country better outside the government. Democratic clubs were appearing in towns and countryside. They claimed the loyalty of Jefferson's warm heart. He could not stay yoked to Hamilton, he said, and serve democracy, too.

It was clear by now that free Americans would always have their differences. They did not live alike. How could they think alike?

From that day on, there were two parties in the United States—and sometimes more.

In western Pennsylvania frontiersmen were felling the forests and planting corn as Washington's forefathers had planted tobacco.

There was one difference. These new settlers were poor people without slaves. Tobacco had been money in colonial Virginia. Corn weighed too much for money. But it could be made into whisky and sent to market on a pack horse's back. When goods were swapped it was used for change. A jug of whisky became money in the western hills.

From this outer edge of the expanding nation, word came to Washington in 1794 that grizzled men in fringed shirts and coonskin caps were reaching for their rifles when a stranger came. It was Hamilton's tax on whisky that was getting them up in arms.

The new government must have taxes to pay its way. This was very clear to Hamilton. To the stubborn mountaineers it was just as clear that they had no money, only whisky. They drove away the tax collectors at gun point. They kept on making whisky, but now by the light of the moon . . . moonshine whisky.

The Whisky Rebellion, Hamilton called it. If the law were not enforced, he said, soon no one would obey the federal government. The strong-willed Secretary of the Treasury went out with a militia force to put down the rebellion. Washington rode with him part of the way. The troops came back with prisoners, who were first paraded through the streets, then flung into a Philadelphia jail.

To see these men in backwoods dress called rebels made the President sick at heart. Some of these rough-and-ready fellows were old soldiers of his. All of them were builders of the American West. They were making a poor living as best they could. He pardoned them—and the Whisky Rebellion was at an end.

As the West was peopled and grew prosperous this trouble would end. But there was another trouble to which Washington could see no end. This was the problem of Negro slavery. It hurt his conscience that in a free country there should be unfree men. He had taken care that his own slaves would be free when he and Martha were gone. What of the rest? "I shall be happily mistaken if they are not found to be a very troublesome property ere many years pass over our heads," the President wrote a friend.

Meanwhile, there was trouble with England again. It set America in an uproar. John Jay was back from London with a treaty. To the Democratic clubs and friends of France, it seemed worse than no treaty at all. England was seizing American ships bound for the French colonies—taking the cargoes and forcing American sailors into her own service. There was nothing in the treaty to stop all this.

Seven weeks Washington waited. Should he sign or not? The cry against Jay's treaty was like the cry against a mad dog. But the only other choice was war. With a heavy heart, Washington dipped his pen and put his name to the hated paper.

"Give us peace for twenty years and then we need fear no country," he said.

The President had to search his heart again when a young student came from France. The student was George Washington Lafayette, his namesake and the son of the man he loved like a son. His father now lay in an Austrian prison, a victim of the wars. Washington longed to open his arms and take the boy into his family.

But Washington was also the President of the United States. By signing Jay's treaty he had given deep offense to France. He dared give no more. For the noble family of Lafayette was no longer popular in that land. Washington had to be content with giving secret help to the young student.

Fortunately, there were family joys to lighten Washington's weariness. The lovely Miss Nelly, now a dark-eyed beauty in her early teens, was capturing the heart of Philadelphia and making ceremonies of official life less dreary. Young Washington was a lovable lad, if not as eager in his studies as his foster father wished.

As his second term drew to a close the President was corresponding with Jefferson and Hamilton. To Jefferson he wrote, as one farmer to another, of peas and clover—and not of politics. Hamilton was now in his own law office. Washington sent him some ideas for a Farewell Address and asked for comments. This time nothing would change his mind.

Chapter 20: FAREWELL AT LAST

THE SKIES were overcast as March 4, 1797, dawned. President Washington, his brow unclouded, hadn't felt so young in years. A burden of care was dropping from his shoulders.

John Adams, about to be second President of the United States, sat by his side. Roly-poly and all aflutter, he looked quite different from Washington, so tall and now so serene. It was as though Washington were saying, "I am out and you are in. See which of us will be the happier."

Although it was the inauguration of Adams, every eye was on the other man. As Washington, now President no longer, left the hall, the crowd pressed to the doors. Outside it swelled into a multitude—a solemn, silent processional.

The man they followed turned for a last farewell. As he waved his hat, a sort of sob rose from the throng. Washington heard the choking sound. Tears streamed down his cheek.

The people's love still belonged to him. The bitter words of the past eight years were forgotten now. A grateful nation wished him well. He had not expected so much.

Six months before, Washington had published his last will and testament to the American people. What he said went something like this:

You are one people, because you have one government. Never let any portion of our country be torn from the rest. The name "American" is more important than any state or local name. Take care the nation is not harmed by extremes of party spirit. Have peaceful commerce with all nations but expect real favors from none. Stay clear of Europe's quarrels and build peace and prosperity in your own land. Good laws under a free government are the happy reward of our cares, labors and dangers.

Washington put these, his best thoughts, into his Farewell Address.

And now he was riding to Mount Vernon with

Mrs. Washington and George Washington Lafayette, the youth whom at last he could treat as his son.

A contented farmer again, Washington returned to the life he liked best. The cider press . . . the gristmill . . . and the fields and fisheries claimed his time. Jolly parties filled the house with laughter. Young people were always about—nephews and nieces and friends of Miss Nelly and young Lafayette. The old general liked to stand in the doorway and watch the gaiety. But if his presence put a damper on their fun, he would quietly slip away.

The guests often stayed overnight, for they had traveled far. Sometimes the girls would come to breakfast with their curls in papers. Two handsome lads galloped up one morning. The young ladies rose to scamper off and fix their hair. Mrs. Washington spoke up sharply. "Stay right where you are," she ordered. "What is good enough for the general is quite good enough for those boys."

She taught Nelly how to manage a great household and how to play the harpsichord. The beautiful instrument was a gift from the general, costing a thousand dollars. Martha made sure her granddaughter got her money's worth by insisting on constant practice.

Letters poured in on Washington, more than he could ever answer. Famous visitors called, more than he had strength to entertain. He found himself nodding after supper. At his age he couldn't ride over his five farms all morning and stay up until midnight, too.

So that is why he asked his nephew Lawrence Lewis to come and be his host and helper. Lawrence was the son of his sister Betty, the one who looked like his twin. One of Lawrence's chores was to sit up with the company while his uncle went to bed.

Welcome news now came from across the ocean. The older Lafayette was being freed from prison. So his son, after being a much-loved member of the Washington family for a year, took ship for France.

A fateful letter followed him on the voyage. Washington wrote it on Christmas Day in 1798. He had to tell the French youth—who was like a son— that France and America were at the point of war. A new government now ruled in France. Much had happened since the Revolution. Now French, not British, were seizing American cargoes on the seas.

Washington wore a new uniform as he wrote the letter. He was commander-in-chief once more and would lead the troops if there were war with France. He had been summoned to duty again in the hour of danger. The French boy's American friends were in uniform, too. Washington Custis was a lieutenant. Lawrence Lewis, a cavalry captain.

But there were some bits of cheerful news to pass along. Miss Nelly was engaged to young Lewis. They were to be married on February 22nd, Washington's sixty-seventh birthday.

It was a big event for the family—with Martha's granddaughter and the general's nephew soon to be man and wife. Washington liked the match, though he had no part in making it.

"Wear your new uniform—the grand embroidered one," Nelly begged as the wedding date approached. With those flashing dark eyes turned on him, how could he refuse her any wish?

But when Nelly came down the winding stairs to the great hall in her bridal gown—he was wearing the worn buff and blue instead.

Afterward, she threw her arms around the general and kissed his cheek.

"You were right," Nelly cried. "I love you best of all in that."

Washington fortunately did not have to command an army again. After a time the war clouds cleared. President Adams sent three commissioners to France to settle the trouble.

In the summer of 1799 Washington wrote out his personal will and testament. Most of the property he left to Martha and their kin, but some was set aside for the education of worthy young Americans. The slaves were to have their freedom after Martha's time. Those who were old or sick were to be taken care of.

Five of the general's nephews were to have the choice, in turn, of his five swords . . . the service sword, the dress sword, the broad sword, the inauguration sword and the sword he wore on Braddock's field more than forty years before. With each sword went a command. "Never unsheath it to draw blood," he said, "except in defense of self or country. But having once unsheathed it, prefer to fall with it in hand than give it up."

His brothers and sisters by now were all gone. "When the summons comes, I shall endeavor to obey it with good grace," he wrote a friend.

Meanwhile, he would be a good farmer. Experts in England were now making a science of agriculture. Washington exchanged many letters with them. He made plans for several years ahead.

These plans were completed on December 10th. They showed how to rotate the crops in every field from year to year to give the land a rest.

Washington rode out to his farms as usual next day. But when he returned the second day a storm had blown up and his hair was full of snow. Tobias Lear, his secretary, suggested a change of clothing before he sat down to the table. This Washington would not do, for the meal was ready.

His throat was sore and bothersome by morning. Deep snow now lay upon the ground. All Washington could do that day was mark out some trees by the river for removal. When urged to treat his cold at bedtime Washington replied, "You know I never take anything for a cold. Let it go as it came."

Before morning he was very ill and could hardly speak or breathe.

Later the sick man sent for Dr. Craik. While he waited he called on Rawlins, the overseer, to bleed him. Dr. Craik, when he arrived, took still more blood, for that was the favored treatment of the day.

The general asked Mrs. Washington to bring him his two wills—and then to burn the one that was out of date. Taking the hand of his secretary he said, "I find I am going. My breath cannot last long. Arrange my accounts and settle my books."

"I hope, sir, you are not so near your end."

"It is a debt that all must pay." Then he spoke to Dr. Craik, his companion on the trip west in 1770. "Doctor, I die hard, but I am not afraid to go."

At ten o'clock that night, December 14, 1799, he told of his wish to lie in the vault overlooking the Potomac River.

"Do you understand?" he asked feebly.

"Yes," said Lear.

" 'Tis well." The general withdrew his hand to feel his own pulse. A moment later the hand fell from the wrist.

Mrs. Washington was sitting at the foot of the canopied bed. In a firm voice she asked, "Is he gone?"

And when she knew he was, she continued, "All is now over. I shall soon follow him."

It would take another book to tell even half the things that were said in praise of the great General Washington by a sorrowing nation. He had shown how, in this new land, a boy who applied himself could reach high goals. He had helped blaze a trail into the great American West, preparing the way for millions to follow. He had heroically defended the frontiers of Virginia in time of trouble. He had improved the crops and encouraged manufactures.

When Americans were called on to defend their liberties, Washington heeded the call of duty once more. He built an army where none existed. Crushing defeats failed to break his spirit. He carried on when everything seemed lost and when nearly every hand was turned against him. He could bide his time, suffer cruel disappointments, strike back with courage and boldness. He kept an army in the field until his country was free. When it seemed as though the new nation might fall apart, it was around Washington that all Americans rallied. He was at the helm for eight years in peace, as he had been for eight years in war.

George Washington was "first in war, first in peace, and first in the hearts of his countrymen." His country, the United States of America, was here to stay.

REAL DATES IN THE LIFE OF
GEORGE WASHINGTON

1732   February 22. George Washington is born in Westmoreland County, Virginia.

1735   The Washingtons move up the Potomac River to the present site of Mount Vernon.

1738   The Washingtons move again. George's third home is at Ferry Farm on the Rappahannock.

1743   Augustine Washington dies, leaving most of his property to his oldest son Lawrence, who is George's half brother. Lawrence marries Anne Fairfax and builds Mount Vernon.

1746   George finds his father's surveying instruments and starts learning to measure land.

1748   Lord Fairfax sends George on an expedition to survey western lands on Virginia's frontier.

1750   George uses his earnings as a surveyor to buy 1459 acres of Shenandoah Valley land.

1751   George sails with his dying half brother Lawrence to Barbados Island in West Indies.

1752   By Lawrence's will George becomes the new master of Mount Vernon.

1753   George becomes Major Washington in Virginia's militia. Late in the year he crosses snowy mountains with a message warning the French to leave the Ohio River valley.

1754   Washington becomes a colonel. He guards the Ohio lands with a small force, and loses the battle of Fort Necessity.

1755	July 9. Washington, as aide-de-camp to British General Braddock, shows great bravery during a disastrous battle with the French and Indians.
1755–58	Commanding Virginia's forces, Washington defends the frontier against Indian raids and sees the French leave the Ohio lands at last.
1759	January 6. Washington marries the young widow Martha Dandridge Custis, and becomes the stepfather of little Jacky and Patsy.
1759–75	Washington manages his plantation at Mount Vernon.
1765	Washington, in the House of Burgesses, hears Patrick Henry attack the Stamp Act.
1769	In protest against new taxes Washington proposes agreement not to buy certain English goods.
1773	Patsy Custis dies.
1774	Jacky Custis marries Nelly Calvert.
1774	June 1. Washington observes day of fasting and prayer as the British close the port of Boston.
1774	September. Washington is sent as one of Virginia's delegates to the First Continental Congress in Philadelphia.
1774–75	Washington takes command of volunteer companies in Virginia to resist British authorities.
1775	June 15. The Second Continental Congress names Washington commander-in-chief of the new American army.
1775	July 3. Washington takes over his command at Cambridge outside Boston.
1776	March 5. Washington fortifies heights com-

manding Boston, forcing the British soon to leave the city.

1776   July 10. The Declaration of Independence is read to Washington's army in New York.

1776   August–December. Washington is forced to give up New York and retreat across New Jersey.

1776   December 26. Washington crosses the Delaware and seizes Trenton.

1777   January. Washington wins the battle of Princeton and goes into winter headquarters at Morristown.

1777   September 11. Trying to defend Philadelphia, Washington loses a battle on the Brandywine River. His new friend Lafayette is wounded.

1777   October 4. Washington unsuccessfully attacks the British at Germantown, but his fighting spirit makes a good impression in France.

1777   October 17. British General Burgoyne surrenders at Saratoga to General Gates.

1777–78 A winter of suffering for Washington's army at Valley Forge ends with the good news that France will help America win her freedom.

1778   June 28. Washington wins the Battle of Monmouth, but the British supply wagons escape.

1780   Fall. Washington learns of Benedict Arnold's plot to betray West Point to the British.

1781   Washington and the French agree on a plan to surround British General Cornwallis by land and sea in Virginia.

1781   October 19. Cornwallis surrenders at Yorktown.

1781	Fall. Jacky Custis dies. The Washingtons adopt his two youngest children.
1783	Peace with England is signed, recognizing American independence. Washington says farewell to his officers at Fraunces Tavern.
1784–87	Washington is a contented farmer again at Mount Vernon.
1787	Washington is chairman of the Constitutional Convention in Philadelphia and works for the adoption of the Constitution.
1789	April 30. Washington is inaugurated as first President of the United States at Federal Hall, New York.
1790	The capital moves to Philadelphia. A permanent capital is planned on the Potomac, near Washington's home.
1793	Washington enters his second term in the presidency.
1793	Washington proclaims neutrality in the struggle between England and France.
1795	Washington signs the unpopular Jay treaty with England.
1796	Washington publishes his Farewell Address.
1797	Washington retires from the presidency and returns to Mount Vernon.
1798	War with France is feared. Washington becomes commander-in-chief again but is not called upon to serve.
1799	December 14. Washington dies. The nation he led mourns and remembers him as "first in war, first in peace, and first in the hearts of his countrymen."

INDEX

Adams, John, 103, 177
Adams, Samuel, 96, 98, 100
Apollo Room meeting, 90–91
Arnold, Benedict, 109, 111–112, 131–132, 136, 143, 145–146, 147
Attucks, Crispus, 96

Braddock, General, 61–67
Brandywine, Battle of, 134
Bridges Creek, 12
Bullskin Creek, 36
Burgoyne, General, 131, 136

Calvert, Nelly, 93–94
Canal project, 158
Cary, Mary, 34
Cary, Sally, 33–34
Cato, 34
Clinton, General, 140–141
Committee of Correspondence, 96
Constitutional Convention, 159–163
Continental Congress, 99–100
Cornwallis, General, 127–130, 148–150
Craik, Dr., 183

Custis, Jacky, 75, 93, 147, 151
Custis, Martha Dandridge, 74–76
Custis, Patsy, 75, 91, 93–94

Declaration of Independence, 115–116
Dinwiddie, Governor, 41, 49–51, 53, 59–60
Duquesne, Fort, 52, 73

Fairfax, Anne, 21
Fairfax, George William, 28–31
Fairfax, Lord, 21, 25–27
Farewell Address, 178
Fauntleroy, Betsy, 36
Ferry Farm, 13
Fraunces Tavern, 154–155
Fredericksburg, 13
French and Indian War, 50–73
French fleet, 143
Fry, Colonel Joshua, 51, 52, 55–56

Gates, General, 136–137
Genêt, Citizen, 171–172
Genn, James, 28–30
Gist, Christopher, 42, 47–48, 54

Grasse, Admiral de, 148–149
Great Meadow, 53–55
Greene, General Nathanael, 148

Half King (Seneca chief), 43–44, 52, 54–55
Hamilton, Alexander, 132, 169, 171–173, 174
Henry, Patrick, 87–88, 101
Hessian troops, 115, 124, 127
Howe, General, 112–113, 115–121, 124, 132, 134, 137

Jay, John, 175–176
Jefferson, Thomas, 169, 171–173
Joncaire, Captain, 45–46

Lafayette, Marquis de, 133, 134, 137, 147–148, 156–157, 167, 175–176, 180
Lear, Tobias, 182–183
Le Boeuf, Fort, 46–47
Lee, General Charles, 121, 141–143
Lee, Richard Henry, 87, 115
Lewis, Lawrence, 180

Madison, James, 159–160
Mason, George, 83, 86, 90–91
Monmouth, Battle of, 140–142
Montgomery, General, 109, 111–112

Necessity, Fort, 57–58
Nicola, Colonel, 152–153

Paine, Thomas, 111, 122
Philipse, Mary, 71
Presidency, 163–178

Rappahannock River, 12, 14
Revolutionary War, 102–150
Rochambeau, General, 146, 148–150

St. Pierre, 46–47
Slavery, 175
Smallpox, 38–39
Stamp Act, 86–89
Steuben, General von, 138–139

Taxation, 86–89
Tobacco planting, 78–79
Trenton, Battle of, 124–127

Valley Forge, 137–139
Van Braam, Jacob, 42, 58
Venango, 42, 45

Washington, D.C., 170
Washington, George
    Youth, 9–24
    Surveying, 25–31
    Heir of Lawrence, 32–39
    Messenger to the French, 40–48
    War against the French, 49–67
    Marriage, 74–76
    Mount Vernon days, 77–84
    Stamp Act, 85–94

Continental Congress, 95–104
Revolutionary War, 105–150
Back to Mount Vernon, 151–158
Presidency, 159–176
Farewell at last, 177–184

Washington, Lawrence, 12, 16, 17–23, 36–39
Whisky Rebellion, 174
Writs of assistance, 86

Yorktown, 148–150

Fort Necessity